COMPOSED ON THE TONGUE

Allen Ginsberg

COMPOSED ON THE TONGUE

Edited by Donald Allen

Grey Fox Press
Bolinas • California

Grateful acknowledgment is made to these interviewers and original publishers:

Lawrence Ferlinghetti and *City Lights Anthology* (© 1974) for "Encounters with Ezra Pound"

Mark Robison and Anonym Press for *Improvised Poetics* (© 1971)

Yves Le Pellec and *Entretiens* 34 (© 1975) for "The New Consciousness"

Paul Geneson and *Chicago Review*, vol. 27, no. 1 (© 1975) for "A Conversation"

Rick Fields and *Loka*, no. 1 (© 1975) for "First Thought, Best Thought"; and no. 2 (© 1976) for "An Exposition of William Carlos Williams' Poetic Practice"

Library of Congress Cataloging in Publication Data

Ginsberg, Allen, 1926-
Composed on the tongue.

1. Ginsberg, Allen, 1926- —Interviews.
2. Poetics. I. Allen, Donald Merriam, 1912-
II. Title.
PS3513.174Z5 811'.5'4 79-21115
ISBN 0-912516-29-1 pbk.

Contents

COMPOSED ON THE TONGUE

ENCOUNTERS WITH EZRA POUND

Journal Notes

Sept. 22, 1967. Drive up to Rapallo from Bogliasco on super bridge across green-castled canyons, bright day and blue water between railroad and hedged cypress—

Pound rose from garden chair as we rounded path from the road surveying downhill large red house gardened. We sat, drank wine under a tree, I opened Indian harmonium and sang Hare Krishna. In the house he spoke, at Olga Rudge's prompting,

"She asks, do you want to wash your hands?"

So then no more speech, except "too much" of the white plate of pasta almost eaten, and chicken/ham broiled, in a plate, he drank white wine— "Too much." O. Rudge lady peeled the grapes, or washed them in crystal bowl. "Too much," but set on a plate he reached out aged pink fingers, thumbnail white frayed.[1]

O.R.: She felt too bad to go to Montreal, woke that night ill, cancelled airplane, sent telegram Montreal, E.P. had said "I won't go without you." Tornado in Milan, planes late anyway, might've missed London connection—

The *Book of Changes* in Italian. Pound had a copy, and the coins were loose in a tiny alabaster bowl Olga Rudge showed.

"If this atmosphere (blue Rapallo and Torquello Bay to Portofino under mountain verdure on promontory below daylit distance) is fine enough for Ezra Pound then these young men, who come to see Pound territory, should try to look at it . . . take time . . . "

"Zoagli" of *Cantos* is town other side of mountain south of Rapallo.

Stared in tiny pupiled eye, he blinked twice, our eyes shifted aside, I meditated.

Later sang, Prajnaparamita Sutra, eyes open on him, eyes

turned away, he shifted back to gaze direct.

After lunch we drove to Portofino—he silent in car—ivory handled cane at side—sat on the quai, he drank iced tea. Long time quiet. Ancient paranoid silent—

"Did you ever try hashish all these years?" I was curious. He looked at me, blinked eyes, shook thin white-bearded cheeks, no, twice—

"Swinburne the only miss . . . he'd a been the one to turn you on," I murmured to myself half aloud.

10/3/67. I went to bed last night, thinking to consult dream worlds as I have neglected to record dreams for a year or two now.

10/7/67. Dream

In large hotel Europe, wandering down twilit corridor having seen Pound—thin beard and stark face upswept hair from *Observer* photo—I am ruminating over his silence, walking along polished marble Italian floor—thinking also to tell friend Ettore [Sottsass] to send Pound photos taken at Portofino us sitting together silent at café waterfront table— Tell Olga Rudge I want to publish photos, money given to poets, or to C.O.P. [Committee on Poetry, Inc]—or I'll tell her myself and ask if it's all right—ruminating in the dream about newspaper publicity— I go out on balcony and sit alone in obscurity after sunset on deck chair—*His silence unhappy*— I begin to sob and then many sobs come and tears wet my closed eyes— I open eyes and see maid with dry mop cleaning the balcony, and another lady in deck chair watching me cry, I am pleased that someone heard me cry, wonder if she understands why— I get up to leave—wake in front room Milan crash of trolleys on tracks 5 P.M. afternoon, my eyelids wet.

10/21/67. Arrived Venice—settled in Pension-Cici near Salute, consulting map on wall, turned saw Olga Rudge and then Pound emerging from dining room. We sat for coffee. Mrs. Rudge explained I wouldn't have had trouble finding their house, "oftentimes Venetians will walk half a mile to show you a tiny alley."

Pound spoke up, "Forty years since I've seen anybody do that . . ."

"Do what, Ezra?" she asked.

"Take the trouble to walk you along to show you the way." He said no more that hour; I arranged to come to lunch next day.

10/22/67. Going to Pound's house—how old?— "How old are you, old man?" I said, several wines and a stick of pot midway between meal.

"82 in several days," he said. That's all he said—all day, with the Italian-Ivanchich speaking of the Afric desert simultaneous—"82"—and I smoked at front of fire, smoked and spoke, and no one reproved me in Venice—perfect balanced, the consciousness—played him "Eleanor Rigby," and "Yellow Submarine," and Dylan's "Sad Eyed Lady of the Lowlands" and "Gates of Eden" and "Where Are You Tonight, Sweet Marie?" and Donovan's "Sunshine Superman." I gave Pound Beatles, Dylan, Donovan—the experts suave and velvet for Futurity— I walked silent out Vio where meets the Grand Canal— I gave Beatles, gave Dylan, gave Donovan—to listen? Forever—tomorrow give Ali Akbar Khan.

[added later]—(Above note written blind drunk Sun. night 1 A.M. returning from Harry's Bar.)

What follows is sober recapitulation days later of what happened Oct. 22.

All afternoon, lunch and wine and upstairs conversation with Ivanchich visiting and Pound silent. I lit a stick of grass at lunch and smoked it, saying nothing about it.

Later high, as I played him music; he had come upstairs swiftly when I asked him to listen, and folded self in chair, silent hands crossed on lap, picking at skin, absorbed—occasionally with a slight smile—at "Eleanor Rigby." "No one was saved" and "Sweet Marie" "six white horses/ that you promised me/ were finally delivered/ down to the Penitentiary." I repeated the words aloud, in fragments—for him to hear clearly. So he sat. "Is this all too much electric noise?" He smiled and sat still. "I just want you to hear this *other*"—and I continued playing, "Gates of Eden," and even "Yellow Submarine." Sat there all along, I drunk, he impassive, earnest, attentive, asmile.

Also that day I chanted mantras to Krishna, and Tara, and Sarva Dakini, fragment of Allah, and *Om a ra ba tsa na de de de de* to Manjusri, describing His book and flaming Sword of Intelligence— Olga hearing Manjusri downstairs came up to top floor where we were (Ivanchich and Pound) and said "It sounded lovely down there" so sat and listened—I was drunk.[2]

A finality "that binds things together." Depression all last week—read papers and *Time*—read *Cantos*, feel better.

10/28/67. Supper at Cici, Olga and Pound at table, "You like the Beatles records? . . . or too much noise?"

Silence.

"You mean those discs?" he said.

"Yes."

Silence.

"No! No!" to the waiter offering zucchini also with sliced mutton.

"Oh yes, take some zucchini, it is good for you—" Olga.

"You liked the Noh, heard first time at the Sanctus Spiriti Church?" Olga asked. He stared thinking, then shook head No, slowly, added "Palladio's theater—"

10/28/67. Lunch w/Olga Rudge, Pound, Michael Reck, Peter Russell. 1:30 P.M. Pension Cici 22 Salute Oct. 28, 1967—

Pound ate, fish, mostly silent during meal, others conversed, he responded occasionally with head nods—re a performance of Monteverdi (?) at S. Friari—

I had one question (being told he responds to specific textual questions from the turn of century—memorabilia)—

That I had found the "place of Carpaccio's skulls"—but where's the place where

"in the font to the right as you enter
  are all the gold domes of San Marco"—?

He looked up and in even, tho high voice, said "Yes, when the font was filled—now they've changed it—used to be like that—"

For yesterday I'd looked in that same holywater basin, a stone bowl, but "for some sanitation reason" as Olga R. added a few minutes later, they'd placed a copper round-rim lip on inside of bowl, for water—and no longer filled the center of the bowl, just the metal canal around the rim.

"I walked half a mile yesterday," I added, "looking for the spot in Dei Grecii, in San Georgio—finally looked in San Marco."

"It used to be like that—the center was filled with water, and the reflection had the domes," he explained. Perhaps less extensively.

"And the 'casa que fue de Don Carlos'—the house that used to be Don Carlos'?"

"That is on the way to San Vio."

"But I've been there—is that near the English church?"

"That's on the corner where San Vio meets the Canal."

"But Salviati's is down the street here at the end—the sign."

"Salviati was in another place in that time," said Pound.

"Oh—but *who* was Don Carlos?"

"The *Pretender*."—he answered.

"So the house is on the corner of San Vio & Canal?"

He nodded, yes.

I continued—explaining that there were a great many specific perceptions—descriptions—of exact language composed—throughout *Cantos*—"tin flash in the sun dazzle" and "Soap-smooth stone posts"—and added I'd gone to San Vio looking for the soapsmooth stone posts— Were they on the bridge to the private door off the square? or the posts at the end of the quai at the canal-edge, or the plinth at the center of the square? Which was it, because they were all rough—changed perhaps—replaced. "Was it a specific stone post you had in mind, or just all the stone posts?"

"No, general—" he said, or nodding negatively, not a specific one.

A few moments silence while I looked thru my notebook for a phrase. "I've been trying to find language equivalent for that light on water—yesterday I arrived at this—

'Leaped on Vaporetto,
    sun yellow in white haze, Salute's
silver light, crooked-mirrored on the glassy surface' "

and repeated to him, while he looked me in eye—fine blue pupil—"light, crooked-mirrored on the glassy surface," and smiled at him. "You approve of that?"

"That's good," he smiled back—hands steady on the table, with almost invisible tremor, white hair straight back above high-slanted forehead—his skin wrinkled at wrists and back of hand, dry, slight white flakes of dead skin, fingernails whitened by picking or rubbing, membrane-white roughness scraped on surface of thumbnail—clean skin of face and brow, with slight flaking of age (not dandruff) but dryness of skin surface under the thin white straight hair above his brow.

Had been talking with Reck about Buddhism, meditation,

mantras, last night at supper and today earlier—and continued the conversation into Pound's ear, leaning toward him talking quietly—Reck's child, Mickey, playing with 14 postcards distracted him, Russell conversing with Olga Rudge at other side of Pound, she at end of table.

Reck asked, "You ever meet Kitasono Katsue?"

Pound, "No." Reck described meeting with Katsue, whom he found clerkish.

Sometimes at table—conversing w/Reck, who on basis of previous night's conversation (Reck'd noted there were Taoist elements in Confucian tradition at origin) was encouraging open discussion of Oriental heresies, asked about Indian gods—in relation to Greek— I had mentioned Vedic Hymns, asking Pound if he'd ever heard Vedic chanting—

"No"—shook his head, he hadn't— I continued, referring to UNESCO new volumes of Hymns to Surya (Apollo), Rudra (Thunder God)—also mentioned Ganesh Chant (White Yajur Veda).

So explained to him—"You remember I was telling you about hearing Blake's voice—?"

He hesitated and then pursed his mouth, nodded up and down slightly, looking away.

"But I didn't tell it coherently."—so described to him the occasion— "a series of moments of altered modes of consciousness over a period of weeks, etc."—ending "no way of presenting that except thru things external perceived in that state" and so continued explaining how his attention to specific perceptions, & WCW's "No ideas but in things" had been great help to me in finding language and balancing my mind—and to many young poets—and asked "am I making sense to you?"

"Yes," he replied finally, and then mumbled "but my own work does not make sense." [or "but I haven't made sense."]

I had asked him before if he would like to come to give a reading in the U.S. at Buffalo or S.F. say, he replied, "Too late—"

"Too late for what—for us or for your voice?" I laughed, and continued, explaining my and our (Creeley, etc.) debt to his language perceptions—speaking specifically of the sequence of phanopoeic images— "soapsmooth stone posts"—even his irritations and angers characteristic, humors, dramatic, as manifest in procession as time mosaic.

"Bunting told me," said Pound, "that there was too little

presentation and too much reference"—referring to things, not presenting them.

I replied that in the last year [Basil] Bunting had told me to look at Pound because *I* had too many words, and showed Pound as model for economy in *presentation* of sensory phenomena, via words. I went on to describe recent history of Bunting—I'd before asked him if he'd seen *Briggflatts* and he had nodded, swiftly, affirmative. So Pound's work, I concluded to him, had been, in "Praxis of perception, ground I could walk on."

"A mess," he said.

"What, you or the *Cantos* or me?"

"My writing—stupidity and ignorance all the way through," he said, "Stupidity and ignorance."

Reck had been adding "encouragement" in general terms, and here said, "But the great lesson has been in prosody, your ear, which everyone has learned from . . ." and described also effect of Pound on Hemingway and Hemingway on Bengali writers—Babel—or Japanese— "Did you," Reck concluded "teach Hemingway?"—as a question to which Pound was silent—doubtful? I opened my mouth to continue the communion—

"Direct presentation"— "Yes," said Reck, "No adjectives"—

Turning to Pound, Reck continued, "your poetry's shockingly direct."

"It's all doubletalk—" Pound re *Cantos* answered.

Reck— "But you have a marvelous ear, one can't praise that too much—great ear— It's hard for you to write a bad line."

Pound— "It's hard for me to write anything."

Reck— "Your reading has been so extensive, and led people to many areas."

Pound— "Not enough . . . I didn't read enough poetry."

Reck— "What you did read you made good use of." . . .

"For the ear—[William Carlos] Williams told me," I continued, "in 1961—we were talking about prosody, I'd asked him to explain your prosody to me—in general, something toward approximation of quantitative—anyway Williams said, 'Pound has a mystical ear'—did he ever tell you that?"

"No," said Pound, "he never said that to me"—smiling almost shyly and pleased—eyes averted, but smiling, almost curious and childlike.

"Well I'm reporting it to you now seven years later—the judgment of the tender-eyed Doctor that you had a 'mystical ear'—not gaseous mystical he meant—but a natural ear for changes of rhythm and tone."

I continued explaining the concrete value of his perceptions manifested in phrasing, as reference points for my own sensory perceptions— I added that as humor—HUMOR—the ancient *humours*—his irritations, against Buddhists, Taoists and Jews—fitted into place, despite his intentions, as part of the drama, the theater, the presentation, record of flux of mind-consciousness. "The Paradise is in the desire, not in the imperfection of accomplishment—it was the intention of Desire we all respond to—Bhakti—the Paradise is in the magnanimity of the *desire* to manifest coherent perceptions in language."

"The intention was bad—that's the trouble—anything I've done has been an accident—any good has been spoiled by my intentions—the preoccupation with irrelevant and stupid things —" Pound said this quietly, rusty voiced like old child, looked directly in my eye while pronouncing "intention."

"Ah well, what I'm trying to tell you—what I came here for all this time—was to give you my blessing then, because despite your disillusion—unless you *want* to be a messiah—then you'd have to be a Buddhist to be the perfect Messiah" (he smiled)— "But I'm a Buddhist Jew—perceptions have been strengthened by the series of practical exact language models which are scattered thruout the *Cantos* like stepping stones—ground for *me* to occupy, walk on—so that despite your intentions, the practical effect has been to clarify my perceptions—and, anyway, now, do you accept my blessing?"

He hesitated, opening his mouth, like an old turtle.

"I do," he said—"but my worst mistake was the stupid suburban prejudice of anti-Semitism, all along, that spoiled everything—" This is almost exact.

"Well no, because anyone with any sense can see it as a humour, in that sense part of the drama—you manifest the process of thoughts—make a model of the consciousness and anti-Semitism is your fuck-up like not liking Buddhists but it's part of the model as it proceeds—and the great accomplishment was to make a working model of your mind—I mean nobody cares if it's Ezra Pound's mind—it is a *mind*, like all our minds, and that's never been done before—so you made a working model all along, with all the dramatic imperfections, fuck-ups—anyone with sense can always see the crazy part and see the perfect clear lucid perception-language-ground—"

He had nodded a little when I said "Nobody cares if it's Ezra Pound's mind"—and I added, and "so, fine, it's Ezra Pound's mind, a fine mind but the important thing, *a model of mind process*— Gertrude Stein also made one, usable—yours however, as I've experimented in transcription, the nearest to a natural model—a model *from Nature*—as Cézanne had worked *from* Nature, to reconstitute the optical field perceptions . . ."

It may have been at this point that he said, as recorded above, that his worst mistake had been "the stupid suburban prejudice anti-Semitism"—

and I responded, "Ah, that's lovely to hear you say that . . ." and later "as it says in *I Ching*, 'No Harm.'"

Sometime in this conversation he'd concluded, "I found out after seventy years I was not a lunatic but a moron."

And I paraphrased "Beginning of Wisdom, Prospero," and was continuing— Reck turning aside from his child asked me to repeat what Pound'd said, which I did and turned eyes to Pound, remembered I'd quoted epilogue verses *Tempest* last Sunday, so repeated them again to Pound, saying "You remember?

Now my charms are all o'er thrown,
And what strength I have's mine own,
Which is most faint. Now 'tis true
I must be here confin'd by you,
Or sent to Naples. Let me not,
Since I have my dukedom got
And pardon'd the deceiver, dwell
In this bare island by your spell;
But release me from my bands
With the help of your good hands.
Gentle breath of yours my sails
Must fill, or else my project fails,
Which was to please. Now I want
Spirits to enforce, art to enchant;
And my ending is despair
Unless I be reliev'd by prayer,
Which pierces so that it assaults

Mercy itself and frees all faults.
As you from crimes would pardon'd be,
Let your indulgence set me free.

He looked at me in my eye kind smiling, I looked at him and then (must've been at this point) asked if he'd accept my blessing —more conversation—the sequence at this hour later inexactly rememberable— We rose, he got coat cane and Olga gave him grey wool small-brim'd hat, walked all of us out on San Gregorio by small canal lined with iron rail—started walking, still talking up street to his alley— T.V. cameramen waiting, a black cable snaked from his door to powerline across alley—and at door we all stood, he outside still while Olga went in— So took him by shoulders looked in his eye and asked "and I also came here for your blessing, and now may I have it, sir?"

"Yes," he nodded, "for whatever it's worth—"

"And more, and more," I said, "I'd like you to give me your blessing to take to Sheri Martinelli"—for I'd described her late history Big Sur, eyes seeing Zodiac everywhere hair bound up like Marianne Moore—which gossip perhaps he hadn't even heard— "To at least say hello to her, I'll tell her, so I can tell her," and stood looking in his eyes. "Please . . . because it's worth a lot of *happiness* to her, now . . ." and so he looked at me impassive for a moment and then without speaking, smiling slightly, also, slight redness of cheeks awrinkle, nodded up and down, affirm, looking me in eye, clear no mistake, ok.

Then he stood, silent, Peter Russell said adieux, I waited, talked to Olga while, "It's horrible, so many come and ask him if he's still writing—" she had said at table; there were now enough *Cantos* for new volumes, scattered and as yet uncollated or edited whatever—"to ask him if he's writing—of course it's different with someone like yourself, to discuss as fellow"—fellow professional or something. "Well it makes him self-conscious"—"Yes self-conscious," she agreed to that language exact— "But if you wait," she had said "and have patience, he needs to talk—he thinks all his work so bad—whereas when he reads it into tape, you can tell he reads with enthusiasm, some parts—other parts, of course, he dislikes but that's natural, after years to be self-critical, anyone would . . ." She spoke very sensibly, explaining how she viewed the apparent perplexity as it was made more difficult by outside uncomprehension of the nature of his present alertness and character.

Then he turned to me— I had kissed him on right cheek—held my hand, and said "I should have been able to do better . . ."

"It was perfect," I replied— "I haven't properly yet sung Hare Krishna to you either . . . I'll be around a few days more anyway maybe . . . see you . . ." He stood then at his door, hesitating to enter—waved down the alley, I walked away with Reck and Russell, who suggested I try to transcribe details of the conversation while it is still fresh to ear.

His remarks several days ago "82 in several days" exact to this Monday Oct. 30. his birthday.

10/29/67.—12 P.M.— Out on Salute boat-station waiting for vaporetto, Peggy Guggenheim with two tiny dogs and Paolo art friend, met gossiping, I related some of conversation with Pound day before—she thought his wartime activities "unforgivable" . . . also asked me if I'd written poem called *Howl* and another poem "Gasoline"? Olga Rudge and Ezra Pound appeared on the floating platform— 9 P.M. dark—she said they were going to Carmini Church for Vivaldi concert, five year celebration of priest, a lady friend singing that night—social appearance—I asked "May I come" and as she said, "Certainly," we went on vaporetto—

Sitting on bench behind them, addressed her and Pound's ear, told story of Julius Orlovsky, as Manichean who wouldn't speak for 14 years because he believed all the evil in the universe issued from his body and mouth. "Are you a Manichean, Ezra?" she laughed. No answer. Walked long time, slightly lost in alleys past open flagstone campo S. Margherita to church (I'd visited it earlier today on walk starting from Zatteria, when I'd met Pound in afternoon sunlight, blinking, waiting on Fondamenta [quai-waterside, facing Juidecca] with Olga for film crew trailing them —standing then in bright clear light long sun yellow rays bathing the buildingsides— I wanted to stay get in the picture, but said I was taking walk, so continued on my way and left them in group with TV director, a large serious artistic looking Italian— I walked several hundred feet on and stepped out on a swaying wooden jetty, sat crosslegged, and watched from distance, as their group slowly ambled back to San Gregorio).

Evening now, we three went into S. Maria Del Carmelo—wrote note there, sitting behind Pound—

Carmini, organ, apse brilliant yellow
gilt angels, violincello,
Byzance cross hung silhouette,
Flowers on altar, Pillars wrapped in red velvet—
old man sat before me,
brown canvas shoes, one heel raised alert,
hat and cane in hand
Smooth woodslab resting
under a fold in his coatback—
white cheek beard dyed red by
velvet light,
black not entirely faded from
back of his skull,
fringed with grey hair,
candle gleam through white web.

Some very delicate Vivaldi violin beginning soft and rising—Olga, Pound following, walked forward along pillared candle-lit left aisle to look closer to her singing friend, they stood there listening to the end. Then without waiting for next pieces of concert to finish, headed home thru alleys, walking—silent awhile, then I began again—as I'd been to look, today, at "lacquer in sunlight . . . russet brown . . . lions out of benevolence," to the left of San Marco (Olga on vaporetto had pointed out House of Don Carlos—other side of San Vio Campo, on corner—Questioned where Salviati's had been, Pound didn't answer)—he didn't respond either, to reference to the lions; anyway it wasn't a question.

I began: "I've been thinking about problem you raised yesterday, the *Cantos* a mess—If they made a static crystalline ideological structure, it would be unresolvable, now. But it is an open-ended work, that is, epic, 'including history,' of movement of your mind and record of focused perceptions, existing in *time,* and changing in time, anything you write now will refer back to the beginnings and alter all that went before—like turning a Venetian blind. Same thing as in Lombardo's Sirens. Beginning back in time with serpent tails, going thru transformation thru Breast *Pisan Cantos* poignancy—ending in present time sculpting clear human eyes. In short, what I'm saying is,—Einsteinian changing universe is recorded, not static crystal shit model—so *anything* you do now is OK and will be proper, appropriate, as means of altering preceding thought-flow by hindsight— Am I making sense?" This addressed to problem of finishing *Cantos*.

Replied, "It's all tags and patches."

I explained lots more, in answer, ending, "I've read *Cantos* through this month and in each canto there's always some condensed perception concrete image round which the other tags, ideologies, irritations and projections and references revolve, so whole work has solid vertebrae." Then continued, "Is your problem one of physical depression that keeps you from recording and registering these final perceptions—whatever you are *now*?"

"The depression's more mental than physical," Pound answered.

Later in conversation I said the *Cantos* were solid—good as Dickens' *Bleak House* I started reading, that was full of exaggerations—said I'd read *The Pit* lately, Frank Norris, had he read it ever?

"No."

So I described the roar of wheat trading on the floor of the Stock Exchange. We got to house, after more on *Cantos*, he not replying, but when he entered his house he said immediately,

"It's too hot in here."

Olga built a fire. I sat down, and next described effect of his poetry on younger poets— Do you know the enormous influence you've had? I asked—

"I'd be surprised if there was any," he said dubiously, looked down, but interested— I recited a few short poems of Creeley, talked briefly of Olson, Wieners—asked him if he knew Creeley's work at all, he nodded up and down, thin beard affirmative. "But do you understand the influence your writing had been as a model for whole generation of younger poets—that is my age half yours now 41 and say Creeley?"

"It would be ingenious work to see any influence," said he.

Explained the influence WCW, Zuke (Zukofsky), Bunting, etc. Said that at first, myself of Paterson, I'd found WCW more usable—

"*Williams* was in touch with human feelings . . ." he said, nodding his head slightly in disgust at himself. I explained it was the practical matter of listening to "I'll kick yuh eye." And I went on explaining the models we had—that Williams didn't have Fire Excitement— Crane had—did Pound know Crane's *Bridge*?

"No." I was surprised, so recited several verses of "Atlantis" comparing it to Shelley's "Ode to the West Wind," and Pound's own anger-inspiration rhythm Canto XLVI "*helandros kai heleptolis kai helarxe*." Asked if he'd tape-recorded that, he nodded No.

Olga served Ovaltine, brought me copy of Canto CX, "Has Mr. Ginsberg seen this?" I said I'd return it, she asked him to sign it for me—he hesitated long time, and said:

"Oh, he doesn't *want* it."

"Well, yes sure, I do," I pointed my finger, "if you want to check your perceptions. I absolutely do."

So he signed, "Alan Ginsberg—dall'autore— Oct. 29, 1967 Ezra Pound."

At home, I also at one point asked him if he was at all familiar with my poetry, he shook his head negative. I said, Well, oddly, it might even please you. This led on to discussion of his influence on younger poets.

10/30/67—3:30 P.M.— Met Pound by Teodoro's statue, cafe there, with Ivanchich and girlfriend— Ivanchich had invited me to lunch at Malamocco's, Pound's birthday today—conversation about Huxley, re electronic spying, I repeated notion that best antipolice state strategy was total exposure of all secrets, rather than electronic monopoly-control of classified information—i.e. unclassify everybody's private life, President Johnson's as well as mine—thence conversation re intrusion of machinery universe—Olga asked Pound for old quotation, which he repeated complete after her fragmentary reference, "As for living, our servants can do that for us."

As habitual, he hesitated over choice of foods, refused vegetables— I gave him 1½ stringbeans from my side dish, which he picked up with fork and ate—toasted him and drank wine, he at first didn't respond, then swiftly took his glass and drank.

I talked a great deal about modern use of drugs as distinct from twenties opiate romanticism (as I saw it)—turned finally and asked him again— "Does all this make nonsense to you now—'immortality pills' and all?"

"You know a great deal about the subject," he replied.

Ivanchich identified Olga's reference to the can of opium

Pound brought— Was it Hemingway's story or Williams'—to friend (Forrest Read?) Ivanchich saying it was in *Movable Feast.* Pound commented:

"Hemingway had the correct version."

Olga asked me if I knew Michaux,—then asked Pound if he remembered Michaux— Pound shook head No, she said, "Oh, you must remember, he came to lunch with us in Paris two years ago" . . . she had described him as very charming.

I had also asked, earlier, if Pound had not ever *met* Hart Crane, he shook head No.

Walked back slowly along Riva Schiavoni, on top of white bridge (Ponte de Pieta across from Sighs Bridge by Ducal Palace) Pound in brown wool hat, St. Georgio Maggiore dome and tower above his head silhouetted in brilliant yellow-blue afternoon light, few people and many grey pigeons crowded on stone ground—we waited by vaporetto for Olga to check at pastry shop—on the way, passing Teodero's column I repeated,

"Shd/I shift to the other side,
  or wait 24 hours,"

and asked what does that mean, shift to the other side of the column, or cross over to Salute?

"Fantasia," he replied.

"What?"

"Just fantasy."

"I thought meant, shift sleeping to other side of the column of Teodoro, or, maybe, change in life—or just writing *poetry.*"

He was silent.

Olga returning, we sat waiting for vaporetto, asked if Reck'd left copy of *Hsi-yu hu* by Yeh-Lu Ch'u-Ts' Ai (Tr. Igor de Rachewiltz, Monumenta Serica, Vol. XXI, 1962). Said Pound's "Immortality Pills" phraseology was from notes in that monograph—also reference to Incense Cults—all Canto XCIX.

At door this evening, returning from an errand, Mrs. Rudge invited me to return later to sing to Pound on his birthday night. Came by at ten attired in silken London-Indic shirt, woven gold, and Buddhist Trikaya emblem round neck—he was silent, by fire (he'd come downstairs)—so chanted *Prajnaparamita Hrydya Sutra* in Japanese and English, then Hare Krishna, and after some birthday cake and a little more champagne, Buddhist Three Vows. Buddham Saranam Gochamee, Dhamam Saranam Gochamee, Sangham Saranam Gochamee. Then in silence still, to illustrate effect of his composition on mine, read—with indifferent voice alas—few pages of "Middle Section of Long Poem on These States." oops! Silence. Eek! Put that down fast after asking, do you see the relationship in method of composition? Silence. So picked up harmonium and chanted 50 verses of Gopala Gopala Devaka Nandina Gopala—high and sweet, and low solemn. Then explained "Gopala means Krishna cowboy" and said goodnight and "Happy Birthday Krishna," he smiled at that. Leaving from door I demanded, "Well, say *Goodnight!*" He nodded amiably, said "Goodnight." So I left.

11/6/67—2:30 A.M. Sun. Night—

Nov. 2, saw Pound on Zatteria, walking at 1 P.M. in sunlight along the stones—Onnisanti Day—asked him "How are you today? Alive!"

He answered, "Worse. And alive."

Several days later met at lunch, he was silent, curious reddish cast to cheeks, observed the elderly waitress carefully bone his fried trout—silent, then swiftly picked up fork, cut a piece and ate. But didn't finish his plate, refused cake and coffee. New clean lavender shirt with wide collar, and monocolored yellow tie. Always hangs his hat outside pension dining room, and his scarf, on brass hook, and carries ivory-handled cane inside to table. Said, "Goodbye, Mr. Pound," and he turned, hesitated, looked at me, smiling slightly, but dumb, shook my extended hand.

Yesterday came down in midafternoon to dining room back of pension kitchen, accompanying Otto Endrenyi—Hungarian-Bolognesi ex-refugee friend of Olga—who'd heard me sing in room an hour earlier—(high with Israeli architect I'd met in flooded San Marco Plaza and we'd walked and smoked his last brown stick of kif, along street from Academia to Zatteria, then up to my room I sang awhile Hare Krishna)— So Otto invited me to coffee—found Pound sitting there alone, Olga at telephone in front office preparing trip to Padua to escape rain floods of early November.

I sat across from Pound at another table, asked him if there was old or classical music to St. Francis *Canticle to Creatures*—repeated question, he answered. "There is no contemporary music." So, high on pot still, I improvised in Hebraic-Indian modes on the complete text of canticle typescript on table before me, with drone harmoney on Peter Orlovsky's brown school harmonium, chanting thru "Frate Morte."

An hour later saw him and Olga Rudge outside hotel, and followed after them with Otto, they to take vaporetto to R.R. to Padua, we to promenade in San Marco at red clouded sunset hour— Pound walked energetically, white raincoat flowing behind him, walked with speedy strength, slowed to climb small bridge-steps to Salute's platform and stepped up firmly, then with youthful balance stepped from the tipsy floating platform onto boatbus and walked ahead into cabin, sat down; vaporetto pulled away from shore, moving upstream.

Morning— . . . empty life, revolving on the surface of a mirror, myriads passing by—

Woke, and realizing late date, only another month and half before reading tour, and fatal time in USA, and I gotta get back soon see Peter, and finish texts once for all, collect books, cash in verbal chips, dropout—all last night at Luigi Nonno's house talk of Cuba and Revolution and Guevara photos on wall and avant-garde collections with machinery, lights, Guevara images fair faced and smiling through boyish beard— Time passing.

Two recollections added September 1, 1979, by Allen Ginsberg:

[1]I asked if he'd ever met Céline, I think Olga said, No. I described visit to Meudon 1961 with Burroughs to see Dr. Déstouches (Céline), and recounted I'd asked which French prose writers he'd liked best. As I remembered he'd mentioned three: C. F. Ramuz, Henri Barbusse (who'd "jazzed up the language") and . . . Paul Morand, one of whose books Céline had liked, his first? . . . I'd forgotten . . . Olga Rudge looked to Pound still bent over his pasta while I was trying to remember, "Ezra, what was the name of that book by Morand you liked so much, you didn't like what he did later . . . " Pound looked up from his plate and said with firm intelligence in perfect French "*Ouvert à la Nuit,*" then bent down his head and continued eating. I don't think he spoke again the rest of the day.

[2]I asked her, later, whether Pound had been pleased or perhaps bored by the Dylan & Beatles songs I'd played for him. Oh no, she replied, if he had been bored he wouldn't have sat there at all, he would have got up and left the room immediately.

IMPROVISED POETICS

[This discussion between Michael Aldrich, Edward Kissam, Nancy Blecker and Allen Ginsberg took place at his Cherry Valley farm, November 26, 1968. Mark Robison published it in a limited edition in 1971.]

Allen Ginsberg: The question is how to figure out where to break the line. Well, here's the problem of writings like the long airplane poem you were just looking at, "New York to San Fran."[1] Since it is written down on a page, silently, without everybody talking, the page determines the length of the line. It's an arbitrary thing—if I have a big enough notebook, it's a big long line, generally, because there's room for the hand to move freely across, and the mind to think freely in terms of, the long line. If it's a little pocket notebook that you stick in your back pocket then you tend to have smaller, choppier lines.

Michael Aldrich: So the literal page you're writing on . . .

Ginsberg: . . . very often determines the length of the line. Now poems like "New York to San Fran" generally fall into paragraphs of short lines which *could* be extended out on the page, when printed, to be like a long line, or a strophe, call it—for lack of a better word—the Whitmanic strophe.

But what also determines where the line breaks is: when the thought breaks. You know, if you are writing in a notebook and--give me a text—writing in a notebook: "Being filled with drum beats and total"[2]—and I didn't know what was going to come after "total," total, total what? Probably it was some sort of Hart Cranian thing like "total ascensions," but that didn't make airplane movie earphone sense—it was total "orchestra shaking Ascensions." So, "Being filled with drum beats and total" on a short page, on a little notebook page, and then indented after that, "orchestra shaking Ascensions"

Then the next line . . . ah . . . what am I referring to? Crane's "migrations that must needs void memory,/ inventions that cobblestone the heart" from "Atlantis" [section of *The Bridge*].[3] So we had "orchestra shaking Ascensions" and that was where the thought broke off, and I had to go back and footnote my thought, so to speak. So the next line was "Crane'd've come to Forever." Now I was interested in the music, so it was "orchestra shaking Ascensions / Crane'd've come to Forever" . . . and then I realized that wasn't really complete, so I put "if he could." [Laughter] So:

Being filled with drumbeats and total
orchestra shaking Ascensions
Crane'd've come to Forever
If he could—

And that's four lines. And since the "if he could" is a subnote on "Crane'd've come to Forever," it's indented below the "Forever" as a modifier of that last line. So the little short phrases there that modify lines before, get hung out on the page a little to the right—which is just normal common sense. A little bit like diagramming a sentence, you know, the old syntactical method of making a little platform and you put the subject, verb and object on it and hang adjectives and adverbial clauses down . . .

Aldrich: Does that affect your reading of the poem?

Ginsberg: Yeah, because actually the mind-breaks that you go through in composing are the natural speech pauses too, or are identical with natural speech pauses: after all, natural speech pauses indicate mind-breaks. This is a really important point. Though the natural speech pauses or breath stops, line stops, and end stops might not fit the way it would sound if someone were perorating, TV platform politics public style and running on, the pauses and stops *would* fit if someone were in intimate conversation . . . uh, saying *uh* hesitating and then completing the little syntactical unit. Just like I just did.

Aldrich: So it's a natural speech rhythm.

Ginsberg: Actually it is a kind of natural speech rhythm that comes when you are speaking slowly, interestedly, to a friend. With the kind of breaks that are hesitancies waiting for the next thought to articulate itself. So actually it was the composing—the breaks in composition with a short-line notebook that wind up functionally, as the equivalent of the way you not only think it out, but the way you might *say* it, if you were talking—at least that's the way I read finally. When I get up and read those units I just make believe I'm trying to think of the next phrase. And then I come out with the next phrase. And so actually that leads the listener, or reader, in an oral interpretation.

Aldrich: Directly imitating the process of composition.

Ginsberg: Yeah, and so it leaves the mind of the reader or listener to be hovering with mine, with the next spurt. And then since the next spurt is always some kind of funny little change, there is always a constant surprise line to line. And the perhaps slight overemphasis of hesitancy on the end stop before the next spurt gives it a dramatic *fillip*.

Aldrich: Now the way I phrase that is, if you are going to read a poem by its white spacing, if you're going to read a poem by the way it's actually physically arranged on the page, you pause every time there's a white space.

Ginsberg: Yeah.

Aldrich: It may not be a very lengthy pause . . .

Ginsberg: Yeah.

Aldrich: Is that generally the way you read poetry?

Ginsberg: Yeah.

Aldrich: Do you pause at the end of a line?

Ginsberg: I pause at the end of a line; or else run-on purposely. So that if someone is reading the page, the text, and hears me read it aloud—and I *don't* pause, but I run-on, the music, so to speak, is in ignoring the possible pause and enjambing. And making a run and making like a fast rhetorical speedy swoop.

In other words, it's just the same thing Marianne Moore does with syllables. Sometimes her line (which is only a count of syllables, in a regulation of the line according to six-syllable, seven-syllable, eight-syllable, two-syllable, maybe . . .), sometimes it requires a pause, but sometimes the charm is that *fillip* where the line ends but the breath goes on, to the next line, so it's like one measure running counter to another and giving it a funny kind of syncopation . . . In the mind's eye if you're reading it and then hearing it spoken aloud on a record. Now you can do either —either pause or don't pause. If you pause, then you've got *that* kind of rhythm; and if you don't pause you've got *another* kind of rhythm.

My basic measure is a unit of thought, so to speak. That's an interesting idea, say, as Williams' idea of a basic "relative measure" for the line. Corso's contribution to the whole thing was that the line was a unit of *thought*, so to speak, which is something I follow. And the reason it's a unit of thought is that's what you wrote down on that line. If you're writing a short line anyway. *So it's not so much a unit of sound as a unit of thought.* But it also turns out that if you vocalize the thought it's also a unit of sound and that somehow or other the squiggles for the units of sound are identical to the squiggles of thought. And they're just as interesting as units of sound as units of thought; if you pronounce them aloud they make a funny kind of rhythm.

Peter Orlovsky: All right, come and get it!

[Lunch break.]

Aldrich: There's something about the difference between the "TV Baby"[4] poem on the page and, for instance, this "New York to San Fran" poem on the page.

Ginsberg: The "TV Baby" poem is like a long blast of rhetoric, with all sorts of language tricks and mind loops going on at one point or another in the poem, in which everything gets mixed up as "a long Train of Associations." But since it is like a train of associations, a train that goes chugging on until it hits high speed, it hits high speed toward the end.

Aldrich: Like a raga.

Ginsberg: Sort of, yes. At the beginning, the strophes or long lines zap along heavily.

it's a long Train of Associations stopped for gas in the desert & looking for a drink of old-time H_2O—
made up of molecules, it ends being innocent as Lafcadio afraid to get up & cook his bacon—[5]

And sometimes they build up and get longer and longer. Now in reading them, they're to be read each strophe as one breath, if possible. However there comes a point about five-sixths toward the end where the lines are slightly shorter and are broken up into halves, like in Biblical apposition or psalmic apposition to the point where:

I am masturbating in my bed, I dreamed a new Stranger touched my heart with his eye,
he hides in a sidestreet loft in Hoboken, the heavens have covered East Second Street with Snow,
all day I walk in the wilderness over white carpets of City, we are redeeming ourself, I am born,[6]

So it's like a series of staccato comes, spurts, within the line. So the breathing there, if read aloud, would be like a heavily labored breathing, with like a gasp for breath after each comma.

Aldrich: With each comma.

Ginsberg: With each comma there. And I read it aloud about three times, so I know now what it sounds like that way. I read it in Buffalo. It works up toward the end where it's like a come, that begins the orgasm, the climax. The climax, literally, is:

Life is waving, the cosmos is sending a message to itself, its image is reproduced endlessly over TV
Over the radio the babble of Hitler's and Claudette Colbert's voices got mixed up in the bathroom radiator . . .
there is a mutation of the race . . . [7]

Aldrich: "Life is waving"

Ginsberg: Yeah, the lines get slightly shorter and shorter till you get to . . . the real climatic moment is I think, "the heavens have covered East Second Street with Snow / all day I walk in the wilderness over white carpets of City" . . . Which for me is the most Shelleyan line. This is absolutely William Carlos Williamsish real, and at the same time there's kind of a spectral thing . . .

From then on "we are redeeming ourself, I am born"—it gets like metaphysical screamings. To a point where—there are some new lines in here that weren't in the original version.

the Messiah woke in the Universe, I announce the New Nation,
 in every mind, take power over the dead creation,
I am naked in New York, a star breaks thru the blue skull of the
 sky out the window, (breath)
I seize the tablets of the Law, (breath)
 the spectral Buddha and the spectral
 Christ turn to a stick of shit in the void, a fearful Idea,
I take the crown of the Idea, and place it on my head, and sit a
 King beside the reptile Devas of my Karma—

And that's sort of like that—Ta da! Trumpets!
And then a little like a coda slightly going down.
Eye in every forehead sleeping waxy & the light gone inward—
 to dream of fearful Jaweh or the Atom Bomb—[8]

And then a little spurt up again,

All these eternal spirits to be wakened, all these bodies touched
 and healed, all these lacklove
suffering the hate, dumbed under rainbows of Creation, O Man
 the means of Heaven are at hand, thy rocks & my rocks are
 nothing,
the identity of the Moon is the identity of the flower-thief, I
 and the Police are one in revolutionary Numbness![9]

Then it goes back to what the original text was. I inserted about eight lines, to make the climax more Messianic. The lines I inserted were lines written about the same time in 1961 in Leary's Newton-Cambridge house.[10] They were referring to the same subject.

Aldrich: That's a good question: when you're going over and back, and reworking for a book, what changes do you make?

Ginsberg: Well, in this book, *Planet News*, part of it is explained in the acknowledgements section. "These poems were printed first (in forms slightly closer to original composition, i.e. there has been some revision for syntactical condensation toward directer presentation—[that's Pound's phrase—*'direct presentation'*]—of the original spontaneous imagery, a method similar to manicuring grass that is removal of seeds and twigs, ands, buts, ors especially ofs that don't contribute to getting the mind high) . . ." So that's like a little short precis on a method of revision as tiny blue-penciling of excess syllables.

Aldrich: Is there ever a time that comes to mind when you change the way that a line is arranged on the page? Meaning, literally, in order to get that syntactic condensation you are talking about?

Ginsberg: Yeah, if it's a short . . .

Aldrich: Or jam a couple of lines that were looser, together?

Ginsberg: Yeah, Yeah. If it's a short-line poem. In some of this *Planet News* I did that, when I found that there was a lot of bullshit in a line, and that two lines could make one line if I put it all together. I did that in a little poem about the Beatles in the Portland Coloseum.[11]

Aldrich: Yes, I know the poem. Do you know the exact lines?

Ginsberg: Let's see what I did with it. I'd have to go back to the original manuscript to see exactly what I did, but I know I changed things. Like "Hands waving *like* myriad snakes of thought" to "hands waving myriad/ snakes of thought." Ah . . . "The million children *of* the thousand worlds," so I just changed "The million children/ the thousand worlds." In other words, I just kept the images and took out a lot of syntactical fat and occasionally put two lines together, two short lines together that had just images in them. I don't know if I can find that . . . Now there's a reason for my putting the words in that order. "bounce in their seats, bash" is one line, and "each other's sides, press" is another. But the way I would read it is: "bounce in their seats bash each other's sides!"—so there isn't *much* of a pause between "seats" and "bash" because you're excited. So you're saying "bounce in their seats, bash each other's sides, press legs together nervous"—all three phrases fast together. So I put "bash" on the same line with "seats" to indicate that the breath should continue. It's really a run-on. And if I said "bounce in their seats," and then in the next line "bash each other's sides" that would be *too much* of a pause, a halt in the rhythm run.

Aldrich: So why not print that on the same line?

Ginsberg: It could be. As in *Howl* form it would be "bounce in their seats bash each other's sides press legs together nervous" in enjambment that would create a run-on effect. It *could* be done that way; alternatively, it could be sounded to get the humor of it, "bounce in their seats, bash/ each other's sides, press!/ legs together nervous" because each one of those is like a little haiku.

Aldrich: —Is a thought, too.

Ginsberg: So to retain the haiku element for the mind's eye, "bounce in their seats, bash/ each other's sides, press/ legs together nervous," I keep them separate. It could be a run-on. But it also could be read run-on with a slight hesitancy after "bash"; so it's "bounce in their seats, bash!/ each other's sides, press/ legs together nervous." Which gives it like three different rhythms running at once.

Aldrich: It's counterpoint.

Ginsberg: Yeah, so you have a counterpoint thing, which is the old use of enjambment, or run-on. In *Howl*, there's that kind of run within the line; there are little breaks within the line, actually, depending on the humor in reading it, too. The short line form as presented just makes it a little more obvious. And since I started out with a little tiny notebook in my pocket going to a Beatles concert, this is the way I wrote it out anyway. But I could have . . . If you notice, in this poem, each *Howl*-type long line would begin at the margin. So it could be "A brown piano in diamond white spotlight" as one single line instead of the "white spotlight" subdependent, indented, from "diamond."

Aldrich: Then what you said, right at the start, about the page size you're writing on controlling the poem's shape and form is really there.

Ginsberg: Yes, Creeley and I had a big long conversation about that, in "Contexts of Poetry,"[12] about how he writes. He was talking about how his writing was determined by the typewriter, neurasthenias of his habit; mine is determined by the physical circumstances of writing, i.e. literally that. And I got that actually from Kerouac, who was that simple and straight about it. If he had a short notebook he wrote little ditties and if he had a long . . . a big typewriter page, he wrote big long sentences like Proust.

Aldrich: That leads to another question I'd like to ask, about the input of the immediate surroundings when you're writing a poem. I noticed in the "New York to San Fran" poem that you were working with inputs such as the movie that was there, the music that you were hearing over the speakers, plus cockpit shuffles, what you were looking at out the window, and there is one point where you take off and really *look* out the window, purposely.

Ginsberg: And also what happens when I go to the bathroom to smoke some hashish and come back. So it's like a collage of the simultaneous data of the actual sensory situation.

Aldrich: Input of the exact moment when you are writing.

Ginsberg: Yes, same thing in "Wichita Vortex Sutra."[13]

Aldrich: Exactly. When you are looking at that later, do you have any selection principle for cutting things in or out?

Ginsberg: Principally cutting out. I do a lot of writing like that, so not all of it is as good, because not all of it is *focused*, not all of it is tied together by some emotional feeling-center. Unless there is an emotional feeling-center with a clear idea, like "I here declare the end of the War!"[14] which is unconsciously present all through that whole "Wichita" composition—from the beginning where I get into a bus with a microphone and say "*all right, now we're going through the middle of America and we're going to dictate a giant poem on the middle of America and the war and everything that is happening*"—so obviously it is Messianic, or could be. It was from the very beginning "Face the Nation," the first line [of Part II]: so "Face the Nation" confronted the Messianism.

Aldrich: I noticed you added another section to the start of it here—why? And what is that from?

Ginsberg: Well, I did that for about a year, running back and forth across the country. The "Wichita Vortex" was the transcription of only one day.

Aldrich: The "Face the Nation" part.

Ginsberg: Yeah—I have similar types of composition, sections ranging over a year, covering the whole country, for a text which is like a whole book, about a hundred and fifty pages.

Aldrich: "These States."

Ginsberg: "A Long Poem on These States."[15] The "Face the Nation" part was coming from Lincoln to Wichita. The proemic part—that's in *Planet News*—is from Wichita to Lincoln, on the way up to Lincoln. It's a shorter piece but as intense. And they make a complementary thing.

And there's other parts published in *Fall of America*. One is from Kansas City to East St. Louis and is the part about Hart Crane—which makes the third section. Then there's another Northwest piece, with Gary Snyder driving the Volkswagen from the Canadian border down through the east side of the Cascade Mountains and down through Pendleton and along the west shore of Pyramid Lake to San Francisco, which is called "Beginning of a Poem of These States."

Aldrich: And hopefully they will all tie together the way that—

Ginsberg: You don't have to hope for it because they naturally tie together; they're all done the same way, during the same time period, by the same mind, with the same preoccupations and obsessions, during the same war. So I mean no matter which way they went they'd all go out from the same brain place. In other words the very nature of the composition ties them together. You don't really have to have a beginning, middle and end—all they have to do is to register the contents of one consciousness during the time period. Hopefully *tie together* in the sense that hopefully the consciousness has a bottom—or a top, or, you know, the consciousness comes to rest somewhere.

Aldrich: Does the Pound language theme run through all of these poems?

Ginsberg: It comes in and out. It first appears in the going up to Lincoln, "language, language/ over Big Blue River." Then it reappears again "Language language/ Communist/ Language language soldiers"—later on it comes in the section to St. Louis, the thing about Senators talk—try to find a language, talk on their feet, saying:

Language, language, uh, uh
from the mouths of Senators, uh
trying to think on their feet
Saying uhh, politely

That actually comes from Pound, not from Kerouac.

In an odd way Kerouac babbles beautiful American name language from *On The Road* in the long section about "Tarpaulin power" on the Wasatch snow peaks or something, just his use of names makes amazing music.

Aldrich: Picking out, well—going across the Midwest and just reading signs is beautiful.

Ginsberg: Yeah.

Aldrich: Here's a question about the spacing, here:

That the rest of earth is unseen,
an outer universe invisible,

Then why indent . . .

Unknown except thru
language
airprint
magic images?

Ginsberg: The way this was determined was: I dictated it on this Uher tape recorder. Now this Uher microphone has a little on-off gadget here (click!) and then when you hear the click it starts it again, so the way I was doing it was this (click!); when I clicked it on again it meant I had something to say. So—if you listen to the original *tape* composition of this, it would be

That the rest of earth is unseen, (Click!)
an outer universe invisible, (Click!)
Unknown (Click!) except thru
(Click!) language
(Click!) airprint
(Click!) magic images
or prophecy of the secret (Click!)
heart the same (Click!)
in Waterville as Saigon one human form (Click!)[16]

So when transcribing, I pay attention to the clicking on and off of the machine, which is literally the pauses, as words come out of my—as I wait for phrases to formulate themselves.

Aldrich: Outta sight!

Ginsberg: And then, having paid attention to the clicks, arrange the phrasings on the page visually, as somewhat the equivalent of how they arrive in the mind and how they're vocalized on the tape recorder. And for that, I have some samples here I can play you—of composition in the car, using the clickings.

It's not the clicks that I use, it's simply a use of pauses—exactly the same as writing on a page: where you stop, you write, in the little notebook, you write that one line or one phrase on one line, and then you have to wait for another phrase to come, so you go on then to another line, represented by another *click.*

On a typewriter I can *see* the space that I can fill up.

Of course, this could be put on one line: "Unknown except thru language airprint magic images or prophecy of the secret heart" . . . Then you could have another line—"the same in Waterville as Saigon one human form." These could be rearranged. But these lines in "Wichita" are arranged according to their organic time-spacing as per the mind's coming up with the phrases and the mouth pronouncing them. With pauses maybe of a minute or two minutes between each line as I'm formulating it in my mind and the recording.

Aldrich: Each pause comes as a click.

Ginsberg: Yeah. Like if you're talking aloud, if you're talking—composing aloud or talking aloud to yourself. Actually I was in the back of a bus, talking to myself, except with a tape recorder. So everytime I said something interesting to myself I put it on tape.

Edward Kissam: So what we're taught to think of as complete thoughts aren't really complete thoughts as much as those kind of bits that come out.

Ginsberg: Yeah. Well if you try—let's see now. How do we *think* is the problem. How do we actually think? In other words this is like a form of Yoga: attempting to pronounce aloud the thoughts that are going through the head. But to do that you have to figure out *how* the thoughts go through your head. Do they go through as pictures? Or do they go through as a series of words, or do they go through your head as full sentences or as phrases?

Now Burroughs doesn't see words—words don't go through his head, *pictures* go through his head. So his method of composition is sitting before a typewriter sort of looking up in the middle distance at the wall, seeing pictures flash through his head like . . . mugwumps seated on a barstool slurping up honey with a long reptilian tongue . . .

Aldrich: And then trying to put that into words.

Ginsberg: And then he simply transcribes it into pictures—*words, picture words.*

Kissam: I was thinking of that formal phrase of yours where you said "a fearful idea," where I wouldn't very easily think of it as a fearful idea . . .

Ginsberg: No, well, the line was . . .

Kissam: "Fearful" even though that doesn't make any sense [it] might be a complete thought . . .

Ginsberg: Yeah. Well, let's see now. "I take the crown of the idea"[17] . . . See like I just said that Buddha is a stick of shit, and Christ is a stick of shit, which is actually not my idea, it's an old Zen koan—Buddha is a stick of shit.

Kissam: Spit on every image.

Ginsberg: No, literally, quote: "Buddha is a stick of shit. The Buddha is a stick of shit," quote unquote, is in Suzuki, as something that somebody said in the fifteenth century, some Zen master—which Gary quoted to me once. So, I say "the spectral Buddha and the spectral Christ turn to a stick of shit in the void"—and then, like, stop for that second, what a weird idea, what a fearful idea—it's a scary idea, "*a fearful Idea.*"

Aldrich: Where are we, what poem are we talking about?

Ginsberg: That's in "TV Baby"—"a fearful Idea." Well it could've arrived in the mind as War! fear—I mean it could have arrived as a shudder rather than as a word or a picture. Or, actually, it could've, it really arrived in the mind as uh . . . gee what would Lionel Trilling say? or what would Pope say, that's kind of a presumptuous rather fearful thing—you can get crucified saying something like that—*announcing* something like that. It is a fearful idea. The shortest portmanteau phrase for that was, "a fearful Idea."

Then, "I take the crown of the Idea," okay, I'll take it on, "I take the crown of the Idea and place it on my head, and sit a King"— And where? "beside the reptile Devas of my Karma—"

Aldrich: A very Medusan image.

Kissam: And there where you go on it shoves it all together. It all happens at the same time I guess.

[End of tape. Conversation resumes later.]

Ginsberg: We're just talking about whether it's written or pronounced on tape. Did you see the long poem called "Beginning of a Long Poem on These States" in *Fall of America*?

Aldrich: I think so, yes.

Ginsberg: It's all about driving through the Canadian border, past Omak and Nespelem and Chief Joseph's grave.

Aldrich: I do remember the poem, yes.

Ginsberg: Well, it's a long thing. *That's* done in paragraphical form. And that was done with a pencil and paper, sitting in the front seat, next to Gary, who was driving, and I wrote down maybe one or two phrases a day—just the key phrases for like, a little epiphany as we passed Omak with "red red apples bend their tree boughs propt with sticks—" so it was just one or two little Rimbaud-like key phrases; then I simply added them, like a tapeworm, one to another—and when I'd get three or four that made an apposition I'd start a new paragraph. So it's maybe one paragraph a day for three weeks. Covering from the Canadian border down to San Francisco. That was *written* in pencil.

That written form is different from tape-poems when transcribed on the page. Though it's written down from the tape recorder, the tape process got me *talking* more—well, I was able to get *more fugitive* things going like "Face the Nation," "You're in the Pepsi Generation," pop signs signalling less, maybe less intense than inner poetizing, but . . . let me show you . . . mental ephemera that I never published . . . over the Rockies . . .

[Break. Discussion moves to sound articulation and Sanskrit.]

Nancy Blecker: Unaaah, it's not so much *yah*, but *nyahh*, *mm-mahh*, thinking of something like you use . . .

Ginsberg: Well, this is Bengali:

> *Jáya Jáya Dévi,*
> *Chára Cháro Sári,*
> *Kúcha-Juga Sóvita, Múkti Hári*
> *Vína Nándita, Pústaka Hástey*
> *Vághabati Bhárati, Dévi Namáste*

Which is like—sounds like a nursery rhyme. Well the thing about Sanskrit is, they—

We have for a beginning, say, to measure a line—we have the possibility of counting the accent, or else we have the possibility of counting the length of the vowel, that is taking into account the length of the vowel, which is the thing I was getting interested in, from hearing the Pound tapes—which you heard, I guess.

Aldrich: No.

Ginsberg: Oh you haven't heard those tapes of Pound?[18] I have them here—I can play those. That's a revelation. Of the musical possibilities of the vowels, or what Pound calls the "*tone leading of vowels.*"

Aldrich: In English.

Ginsberg: Yeah, in English. If you . . . I have a tape of his reading *Con Usura*, With Usury—and the key is in the way Pound vocalizes—"with usura the line grows thick   with usura, is no clear demarcation . . ."[19]

Now this way is accentual:

> du du/da/du du da du da
> with usúra, the líne grows thíck.

But Pound doesn't say it that way. Pound speaks it, "with usura the line . . . grows . . . thick."

Because he wasn't saying *the line gets thick*—he wasn't saying *gets*—he meant *grows* thick, historically, with usura, over a century—will grow, *thicken* the line. So (slower, ponderous):

with usura, the line . . . grows . . . thick . . .
with usura is no . . . clear . . . demarcation

So, in other words, every syllable is intentional. And if it ain't intentional, then it doesn't belong. If it's a filler, then throw it out. From that formulation of Basil Bunting's, Dichten = condensare: to condense. So condense everything down to what you *mean* to say. If you condense it all down to what you mean to say, then you can make a music out of the intentional and significant . . . syllables. And you can *pay attention to the tone-leading of the vowels.* See? It's not pay-attention-to-the-tone, but you can pay attention because EACH THING . . . MEANS . . . SOME . . . THING. And that gives it a density, the line, gives a density to the line.

Now, the Sanskrit thing is even deeper in a funny way, 'cause the grammar is all built on yoga—on a physiological body yoga. So that the first letter would be *a* of some sort or other, but there'd be four or five different kinds of a's apparently beginning at the back of the throat *awhhh* and then there's the *ah* and then there's the *aw* or whatever would come up to the front of the mouth box . . . *a* . . . so it's *awhh* to *a*.

And then *bawhh* to *bee* and *sah* or *kah* to *cee*, and *da* or *duh, thuh*, to *dee* . . . I don't know exactly.

So the mantra formulas have what are called bija syllables, or seed syllables, because their deployment, physiologically in the body during their pronouncing, is crucial—because they have a whole schematic significance that we don't begin to have in our alphabet and in our combinations of the alphabet into word-sounds. In a funny way there's a superhuman onomatopoeia going on in Sanskrit. For instance, one of the mantra-yoga seed-syllables is *dhuh*. (Note: *Dha*, sound is a cross between *duh* and *thuhh*.) The reason is that, to pronounce it, first you have the *the* with the tongue between the teeth, *the*, but then it jumps to the back of the throat, *dhuhh*—and not only to the back of the throat, it jumps down to the middle of the chest to get the *uhh* the dh*uhh*!—so like there's a mantra-yoga singing teacher who was telling me that the next step I should learn, for instance, after doing A-OHM and things like that, is, the famous DUH! sound, because that's the key to suddenly wakening up like a whole Reichian chain of muscular reactions, from the front of the lips to the heart center: DHUH!

And then if you use the *Duh* in combinations with others—with others like, I don't know,—*Dha-Phat!*—you're going through a whole physiological exercise, involving not merely vocal cords but the whole *prana* breathing apparatus.

Aldrich: It's like getting hit in the chest, and you want to go uh!

Ginsberg: Yeah, and especially, it's touching special jujitsu pressure points on the body, by pronouncing them—so it's doing like a physical exercise or a yoga involved with the breathing and also the exhalation of the breathing. Breathing IN to a certain depth and exhaling in a certain way—through the ears or through the nose, or exhaling nasally.

Now the AUM is interesting because—as I've discovered in practice at this point, after Chicago—the *Ahh* is like an open sound, coming up from the center of the body, *Ahhhhh!*—like a sigh out of the mouth—but then the air gets held and imprisoned in the mouth to vibrate the palate and the bottom of the brainpan, skullbone: Aaw-*mmmm*, because the *mmmm* when you breathe it out nasally, actually literally makes a vibration in the bone, around the nasal cheekbone and the palate, which is what is upholding the brain. So what you're doing is setting up some vibration which is giving a massage . . .

Aldrich: Right on the bottom of your brain!

Ginsberg: A thing on the bottom of your brain. And that's why, if you say, AUMMM, AUMMM, for a couple hours, after a while your brain begins vibrating. Or the vibration begins there and begins to affect the whole body, so it must be some physiological-electrical, alpha-rhythm tie-in that gets set up—because if you do that AUMMMM, and you do that *MMMM* for like five minutes, you begin to feel that buzzing throughout your whole physical skull . . .

Getting back to the Sanskrit prosody, if you have a prosody built on *that*, it's so complex—you can do anything with it—it's like having the basic patterns of physiological reactions built into the language, into the alphabet—and then making combinations of the alphabet you can play like an organ, to get different effects.

Aldrich: The body is a literal violin, then.

Ginsberg: Yeah! An interesting statement in the *Bhagavadgita* is, Krishna is pointing out all his different forms and aspects, he's saying among gods I am Krishna, among directions I am, I don't know, the East and among colors I am blue, and "among poetic meters. I am the *Gayatri* meter."[20]

The universal meter is the Gayatri meter, apparently, and so—what is this Gayatri meter? There is the Gayatri mantra which is a very, very famous one, which I don't know all the way through, but it begins:

AUM, BHUR, BHUVAH SUAHA
TAT, SAVITUR, VARENYAM
BHARGO DEVASYA DHIMAHI,
DHIYO YO NAH PRACODAYAT.

It's some kind of thing that's asymmetrical. And once you examine it through, it's not symmetrical, not repeated, but it seems to cover like a whole long free line and be complete. It covers all body sounds possible.

The meaning of it is something about Hail to the first light, that begins all other lights, which is the Female Principle, also, Gayatri, Devasye.

Aldrich: Is that meaning given in the *Gita*?

Ginsberg: No, it's not: It's from another Sanskrit text. Though that *Gita* line is written in Gayatri meter I would guess.

Aldrich: I would think so, yes.

Ginsberg: But the Gayatri mantra is a very famous mantra which all Brahmins know, it's one of the—like when they do Aarti, or worship in the evening, or when they do any kind of a ritual thing usually at one point or other Gayatri meter is one of the things that's pronounced. So. That's all I know about the Sanskrit prosody—which is just a hint that there's this giant, extremely sophisticated and physiologically-based system, that's as complicated as the nature of the human body, practically, or is fitted to the nature of the human body and touches all the key combinations. So probably a study of Sanskrit prosody would take us deeper into what Pound and Williams and everybody—and Rimbaud's alchemy of the word and color of the vowels—had all been hinting at, over the last century or so.

Aldrich: Has your own use of mantra done anything that you can be very specific about, with your poetry?

Ginsberg: Yeah a lot, *now.* Mainly it's made me conscious of what I had been doing with long lines in *Howl.* And . . . made me conscious of what I'd been doing with breathing as in the Moloch section of *Howl,* or parts of *Kaddish*—that the . . . rhythmic . . . units . . . that I'd written down . . . were basically . . . breathing exercise forms . . . which if anybody else repeated . . . would catalyze in them the same *pranic* breathing . . . physiological spasm . . . that I was going through . . . and so would presumably catalyze in them the same *affects* or emotions. That's putting it a little bit too . . . rigorously, but . . . that's the direction.

Doing mantra made me conscious of what I was doing in Poesy, and then made my practice a little more clear, because now I realize that certain rhythms you can get into, are . . . *mean* certain feelings. Well, everybody knew that anyway all along. But some rhythms mean something.

Aldrich: If you're going Dumpty dumpty dumpty dumpty dumpty dum it's different than if you're going daahh, duhhh, dummm, duh-dummm.

Ginsberg: Or, if you're going Bum! ba-ta TUM, BUM: BUM, ba-da-DAA . . . / BOM, bata BOM BOM, BOM bata DAA . . . See, I'm writing a long poem that's got that rhythm now:

DAT- dada- DA- dada
DAT- dada- DA- dada
DAT- dada- DA- didi-da, DON- dada- Da,
DAT- didi, DAAA!

It'd be interesting again—those are like ancient Greek dance Dionysiac rhythms. See, so I get more then . . .

And then, also, the vowel sounds—I've been digging the vowel sounds more, and *the tone leading of vowels,* out of Pound, as Pound talks about it—and that's led onto an examination of Blake. And the single syllable, or the individual syllables, in Blake, and then the possibility of putting them to music. So I'm getting all hung up now, from listening to that line, "with usura the line grows thick," as pronounced by Pound, I begin to get more sensitive to the fact that each syllable in a Blake poem is intentional and therefore has to be pronounced intentionally, as it was meant—like:

Beneath them sit. The aged men. Wise
guardians of the poor.

which means a great syncopation.

Beneath them SIT the AGEd MEN, WISE
GUARDians of the POOR!

Or—

'Un̆seén, thĕy poúr bléssin̆g,'

It's not—

'Un̆seén, thĕy poúr blĕssíng,'

It's—

'Un̆seén, thĕy poúr bléssin̆g.

[Sings:]

Un-SEEN, they POUR BLESS-ing . . .

So by trying to fit them to music, I have to pay attention to the lines in Blake, I have to pay attention to the *intonation* of the syllables, whether they go up or down:

POUR
SEEN, BLESS-
Un- they ing

Or whether they are going up or down emotionally, and musically, and whether they're to be skipped over, or whether they're to be pronounced emphatically, like:

ÁH! SÚN FLÓw̆er

instead of,

> Ắh Súnflŏwér.

In other words it gets me out of the hangup of iambic *stress* into vowel-length consciousness, which is deliberate speaking voice awareness.

Aldrich: Who did the music for the Fugs' version of "Sunflower"?

Ginsberg: Kupferberg and Sanders, mostly.

Aldrich: The actual music, I mean.

Ginsberg: They made up the tune, and somebody wrote it down for them . . .

So I've been going through all of Blake, trying to understand a lot of things I didn't understand before, for the first time—by simply paying attention to what's being said by mouth, on account of I'm having to pay attention to figure out how each syllable would have its musical note as an equivalent. See, otherwise, it would be:

> My mother bore me in the southern wild,
> And I am black, but O! my soul is white;[21]

But—

> My MOTHer BORE ME in the SOUTHern WILD
> And I AM black but O! my soul IS white;

So in other words, it brings more color, intonation, to each syllable pronounced.

Aldrich: And what's your tune for that?

Ginsberg [sings.][22]

Aldrich: In other words, the tunes grow right out of looking at what's on the page.

Ginsberg: Exactly.

Aldrich: My white spacing thing again.

Ginsberg: Well—I'm looking at what's on the page, but to be a little more definite it grows out of being conscious or *aware* of the meaning, intention, or the significance of each syllable on the page—and recognizing that each syllable *has* a place, AND a purpose, when it's really good poetry. When it's sloppy dreamy poetry then there's a lot of syllables that don't have any function—that don't have any *intention*—they're just there because the guy was writing unconsciously and, you know, unconsciously hears the . . . echoes of old iambic quatrains up in the alley or something.

Aldrich: All right: what you were saying a minute ago about Sanskrit, and about Gayatri meter, if that is in fact true, and I'm sure it is; that by pronouncing certain syllables correctly, not meaning correctly in a grammatical sense, but correctly to find the right place in the body where they are to be pronounced from and where they most affect—then that means you can write a prosody, you can write poetry using a prosody even if you can't write about the prosody specifically.

Ginsberg: Oh, yeah! All you have to do is know what they're *saying*.

Aldrich: Which is literally bringing all your physical universe into the thrust of that prosody.

Ginsberg: Yeah. And that's exactly what Olson has been talking about all along as *projective* verse, involving the complete physiology of the poet. That's what he meant.

Aldrich: What does he mean by "The syllable is connected to the mind, but the line is connected to the heart"?—I think that is his schema.[23]

Ginsberg: Well, I don't think he was thinking in terms of AUM syllables; I think he was thinking in terms probably of Marianne Moore syllables being connected to the mind, because you can . . . divide them, like Marianne Moore did, just sort of automatically or arbitrarily—each syllable—five-syllable, seven-syllable lines, then repeat them. But the *line* itself is connected with the breath in that the whole body's intention is mobilized to pronounce the complete phrase (or complete line), in his projective conception. And if the whole body is mobilized, that means the whole single breath of the body is used, whether it's a shallow breath or a deep breath . . . and if it *is* a physical breath it means it's the whole metabolism and the feelings of the body and the *heart* spasm that's involved, so that the breath leads, so to speak, directly to the heart, the center of feeling. At least that's the way I interpret it.

Aldrich: I'm interested in the gossip back of all the starting of that theory—just because I'm interested in that gossip. In Kerouac's *Paris Review* interview[24] he says that *he* started that. So, what's the story?

Ginsberg: Well, I don't think that anybody can claim to have quote "started that" unquote, whatever "that" is—the idea of breath, because . . .

Aldrich: The breath as control and measure of the line.

Ginsberg: Well, it's implicit in Apollinaire, it's articulate in Artaud, in Artaud's cries . . . It's developed, independently and theoretically, by Olson, I presume, from the early 40s, or earlier, out of Pound . . . but Kerouac's most clear use of it, and most available use of it—Kerouac used it in such a way as it became immediately apparent in a way, a popular way. That was arrived at independently by Kerouac in the early and late 40s. So I guess what he means is that he doesn't want to get all involved with complicated literary theories or terminology with which he had nothing to do . . . his is just simple common-sense *practice.* And since I learned mostly from Kerouac, and then put a patina of literary categorization over it later on, having dealt with Williams and Creeley and Olson—though actually I learned the simple spontaneous practice from Jack—without any of the complex labels involved. This is a very simple thing: *talk as you think.* And talk as you talk, instead of talking as a literary person would be taught to talk if he went to Columbia.

I think also Kerouac is very resentful of my trying to make a unified field of his practice, and Olson's practice, and trying to reconcile them all and say it's all one, community effort, when Kerouac *wasn't* exactly working in that large a community, or, you know, I guess he felt more like a private solitary Melvillean minnesinger or something.

Aldrich: Just before *Howl* was written, the only people who were singing, that way, out of themselves completely, out of their bodies, were blacks. And then along came Elvis, and revolutionized white music—"Ah sing thuh way ah fee-ul."

Ginsberg: Yeah. Kerouac learned his line from—directly from Charlie Parker, and Gillespie, and Monk. He was listening in '43 to Symphony Sid and listening to "Night in Tunisia" and all the Bird-flight-noted things which he then adapted to prose line.

Aldrich: How?

Ginsberg: So that Kerouac comes autochthonously—is that the word?

Aldrich: Okay.

Ginsberg: Autonomously from, you know, sitting in the middle of Manhattan listening to the radio and picking up vibrations of a new breath, from the spades, and he *does* give credit there.

Aldrich: And so do you, in the liner notes in the back of *The New American Poetry* anthology.

Ginsberg: Yes. I really learned it from Jack. So—when it gets mixed up with more literary/literate discussions, he probably feels that's getting it too complicated, and it's slipping away from his actual sources. Or I guess he doesn't want to be literally categorized as a follower of Olson's projective verse, because he's not, literally. I mean he's following Charlie Parker, and also following Thomas Wolfe, and Saroyan—and Proust, and Céline, who also has that funny kind of speech extension.

I don't think that Olson would claim that Kerouac was writing projective verse. I think that Olson would say that "projective verse" is his terminology for this kind of writing.

Aldrich: Sure.

Ginsberg: Which is a universal form—rising out of Gertrude Stein, rising in Céline independently in the 20s, rising in Kerouac and Wolfe. Olson really was attempting to formulate it in academic terms so professors could understand it—because that's all they—the only terms they can think in—so he found a categorical, terminological set that people who were hung up on categories could deal with—and he wrote a very literate essay to explain it in literary-essay terminology. Kerouac wrote his "Essentials of Spontaneous Prose," which was written, I dunno. When was the "Projective Verse" essay written?

Aldrich: '50? '51? Fairly early.[25]

Ginsberg: I don't know when Kerouac wrote his "Essentials of Spontaneous Prose,"[26] but that's around the same time, because when I came to San Francisco in 1954, I had it pinned on the wall of my hotel room and Robert Duncan came to look at a little book[27] of poems I had and saw it on the wall, looked at it, looked twice and thrice, and said, "Who wrote that? Who wrote THAT?" because it's so, you know, *right*.

So that was a source of—the development was synchronous—the key is synchronicity, because it was darkly inevitable.

Aldrich: It was coming out of the Head, hair, it was coming out of the universe.

Ginsberg: Just as the return of attention to actual images and observed fact, through Williams, was coming synchronously, at Reed College in '48 with Snyder and Whalen, who'd met Williams, and myself who went to see Williams that same year in Paterson—and in the Berkeley Renaissance.[28]

Aldrich: Can we come back to Williams later? Basically it's his and Pound's sense of meter and music that's at the heart of my white space idea, but I wanted to see what you think about this remark about *Howl*, that I made several years ago.

> —*Howl*, the most famous of his poems, is extremely rhythmical. The meter is sustained primarily by anaphora, the repetition of the same word or words at the beginning of two or more successive verses (lines), clauses, or sentences, a device also used by Shakespeare in Sonnet 66 and by Whitman throughout his poetry (see Sections 31, 33, and 43 of "Song of Myself," for example). To use musical terms (particularly appropriate because the lines of *Howl* use almost exactly the same methods of Charlie Parker's saxophone improvisations), a repeated cadence of anaphoric words like "who" and "Moloch" is taken off from the cadenzas, long swirling patterns of movement. The long line is sustained just because its movement is interrupted recurrently by one unit of that movement.[29]

Ginsberg: Yeah.

Aldrich: A device also used by Shakespeare—throughout his poetry.

Ginsberg: More specifically by Christopher Smart, in *Rejoice in the Lamb.*

Aldrich: To use musical terms—saxophone improvisations—

Ginsberg: Lester Young, actually, is what I was thinking about.

Aldrich: Oh. Okay.

Ginsberg [sings]:

> Dadada DAT DAT DA, dada DA da,
> Dadada DAT DAT DA, dat da Da da,
> Dadada DAT DAT DA, dat da Da da,
> Dadada DAT DAT DA, dat da Da da,
> Dadada
> dadada
> dada da dadah . . .[30]

"Lester Leaps In," *Howl* is all "Lester Leaps In." And I got that from Kerouac. Or paid attention to it on account of Kerouac, surely—he made me listen to it.

Aldrich: A repeated cadence of anaphoric words, like *Who* and *Moloch*.

Ginsberg: *DAH*! da da DAT DAT DA, da da DA da, yes.

Aldrich: Is taken off from, by cadenzas, long swirling patterns of that movement.

Ginsberg: Exactly. Yeah, Dah or Who was a base to return to and spurt out from again. I'm thinking of that little essay I wrote.[31] *Cadenzas* is a nice word. They're all cadenzas beginning with that one note . . . which is like the opera—you know the opera girl studying:

> ah ah ah AH ah ah ah, ah ah ah AH ah ah ah . . . (scales)

Aldrich: What's interesting about that, is that *WHO* is never emphasized.

Ginsberg: What?

Aldrich: *Who* is not accented. It's

> who poverty and tatters a la la la la la,
> who a la la la la la

but the *who* is not,

WHO! poverty and tatters a la la la la la—

it's never accented.

Ginsberg: Well. It's more like—no, it's not. Well the image I was thinking of is the bardic thing—where the bard has his strumming instrument, or his lyre, and gives . . .

Plonggggggggg . . .
And Ulysses went forth on the ships and the ocean
Plonggggggggg . . .
And the next thing they saw was the god Neptune rising up out of an island,
Plonggggggggg . . .
And they went up and crawled on Neptune's beard,
Plonggggggggg . . .

So the *plong* was just something to get your mind going again, or the "Who."

Aldrich [to Kissam, referring to an earlier conversation]: What were you saying about the *nesting* quality of "Who"?

Kissam: I was just saying that the "Who" brought everything, compacted it completely, almost as though it were all written vertically, to have the "Who" there, because syntactically it always brings you back to the start . . .

Ginsberg: Yeah. Like I was doing that one. It's such an easy thing to do, like once you get something going like that you can always come back to the same thing and add another one on.

Aldrich: Well, I think as a rhetorical device that's your most common. You keep doing it.

Ginsberg: Yeah. Whomdoya call it does it also—Smart uses the word "and"—"And let me rejoice with the ass Oneocrotalus whose voice brays like" . . .

Aldrich: That's Greek! That's the Greek *kai*.

Ginsberg: Yeah?

Aldrich: That *kai* is used constantly, and all Greek prose . . .

Ginsberg: The Greek what?

Aldrich: KAI. *Kai* is the greek word for "and"—and they use it at the start of more sentences than not.

Ginsberg: Yeah? *Kai*?

Aldrich: Because it links—it ties it right back into the . . .

Ginsberg: Pound uses it once, in the "*And* they heard the frogs singing against the fawns"—remember that?

Kissam [laughing]: Melina Mercouri uses it in the *Children of Piraeus* [laughter].

Ginsberg: I finally use it in "Kral Majales." "And I am the King of May, and I am the King of May, and I am the King of May"—I didn't know it came from the *kai* though—that's interesting.

Aldrich: Greek.

Ginsberg: Well how did the Greeks use it exactly?

Aldrich: It's Greek prose writing. Half of your Greek prose sentences—well not half, a third, that's still a lot—start either with *kai* or *de*—and it links it, ties it directly back into the sentence previous to it, exactly like a colon or semicolon would.

Ginsberg: Yeah. Or ever the silver cord be loosed,
Or the golden bowl be broken,
Or the pitcher be broken at the fountain,
Or the wheel broken at the cistern . . .

I don't know what that "or" is doing there. It doesn't mean much, except as a rhetorical device to get everything hung in one thought.

Aldrich: It's that conjunction.

Ginsberg: Yeah. Well, what was necessary was a conjunction, or a junction, to link all those rhythmic cadenzas together, that's all.

Aldrich: I noticed the same thing going on—oh—then, in the back of the Allen Anthology[32] you said something about, with the "Sunflower Sutra"[33] you're trying to do the same thing, but without using a "who," without using a specific word repeated as a base.

Ginsberg: Yeah, a lot of times what I try to do is—the important thing is to get that continuous locomotive rhythm going. So with "Sunflower" I simply eliminated the "who," figuring that—now when I was conscious that it was the locomotive rhythm I was after, then I could have one long cadenza that you know, didn't return, didn't interrupt itself by having to return to its base—

And this "TV Baby" poem is like one *giant* cadenza, literally, in the sense that it's all typed out as one continuous, practically all one, sentence that goes on and on, working all day and all night—that builds to a climax, without the need of returning to a rhetorical base. And the ideal would be, you know like, why get hung up on the conjunction. Why not just, you know, do it—the conjunction's sort of like a crutch to start it moving again. And then the interesting thing would be—to fly without crutches.

So like in "Sunflower" I was trying to fly without crutches. Or in "TV Baby," to fly all the way. Same thing also in a lot of *Kaddish.*[34] By that time I was really quite conscious of the fact that the "Who" was a device, an interesting device but I wished that I could do without it and get the thing to—purely speed forward.

Kissam: Do you think the exclamation marks are—whether they're written there or not—as in "Sunflower," where you have to emphasize the first word of a sentence as a—you know—*I* am the king, or say *You* are something—would that be what's doing it there because you have that really *strong* beginning?

Ginsberg: Yeah. You could use the exclamation points as a crutch, too—hang it on the end.

Aldrich: When you say literally "make Mantra of American language now"[35] what do you mean? Do you mean we should literally start chanting the lines for mantra purposes?

Ginsberg: No. No, that's not what I mean. One function of a mantra is that the name of the god is identical with the god itself. You say Shiva or Krishna's name, Krishna is the *sound* of Krishna. It's Krishna in the dimension of sound—so if you pronounce his name, you, your body, is *being* Krishna; your breath is *being* Krishna, itself. That's one aspect of the theory of mantra.

So I wanted to—in the English language—make a series of syllables that would be identical with a historical event. I wanted the historical event to be the end of the war, and so I prepared the declaration of the end of the war by saying "I hereby make my language identical with the historical event, *I here declare the end of the war!"*[36]—and set up a force field of language which is so solid and absolute as a statement and a realization of an assertion by my will, conscious will power, that it will contradict—counteract and ultimately overwhelm the force field of language pronounced out of the State Department and out of Johnson's mouth. Where they say "I declare—We declare war," they can say "I declare war"—their mantras are black mantras, so to speak. They pronounce these words, and then they sign a piece of paper, of other words, and a hundred thousand soldiers go across the ocean. So I pronounce *my* word, and so the point is, how strong is my word?

Well, since Shelley says that the poet's word is the strongest, the unacknowledged legislator's, the next thing is: let the president execute his desire [laughing], and the Congress do what *they* want to do, but I'm going to do what *I* want to do, and now it's—if one single person *wakes up* out of the mass hallucination and pronounces a contrary order, or declaration, contrary state, instruction to the State, to the Government, if *one* person wakes up out of the Vast Dream of America and says *I* here declare the end of the war, well, what'll happen? It was an interesting experiment, to see if that *one* assertion of language will precipitate other consciousnesses to make the same assertion, until it spreads and finally until there's a majority of the consciousnesses making the same assertion, until that assertion contradicts the other assertion, because the whole War is WILL-FULL-NESS, and the War is a Poetry, in the sense that the War is the *Happening*, the *Poem* invented and imagined by Johnson and Rusk and Dulles, Luce, and Spellman and all those people; so the *end* of the War is the *Happening*, the Poem invented by Spock, or myself, or Phil Ochs, or Dylan, or—

Aldrich: Sanders . . .

Ginsberg: Sanders, or A. J. Muste's ghost, or Dorothy Day, or David McReynolds, or Dave Dellinger, or anybody who wishes to make a contrary statement or pronouncement.

Now as I make a pronouncement, contrary to the Government's pronouncement, the question is—I give in to the desire—there's an explanation of that here, to Carroll which he didn't understand, but what I wrote, is:

> Not only a question of legislator as Shelley's formula. Merely that the War has been created by language (as per Burroughs' analysis for his cut-ups) (or Olson's complaint about abuse of language in Maximus Songs) (or W.C.W.'s) & Poet can dismantle the language Consciousness conditioned to war reflexes by setting up (Mantra) absolute contrary field of will as expressed in language. By expressing, manifesting, his DESIRE (BHAKTI in Yoga terminology—'adoration').[37]

Now, my desire is for the end of the war, so I simply say, flatly, "I desire the end of the war"—or I even *declare* the end of the war. So in that sense, make a mantra of AMERICAN LANGUAGE. "Now I declare the end of the war." Make a magic phrase, which will stick in peoples' consciousnesses like a rock, just as the phrase "domino theory"—another phrase that stuck in peoples' consciousnesses like a rock—got them all confused.

Aldrich: The problem seems to be translating that into anything more than your own single power.

Ginsberg: Well, I don't think that's such a problem. See—my own single power in saying "I declare the end of the war" isn't just my *single* power because it represents my desire—it's my unconscious as well as my conscious power. And that desire is archetypal, it saturates half the nation, according to the Gallup poll. Except "What oft was thought but ne'er so well expressed," so why doesn't somebody get up and *say* it? So once somebody gets up and says it, that precipitates the awareness, the same awareness of the same desire to end the war, in lots of other people—or, as Shakespeare says, "One touch of nature makes the whole world kin."

So it's a question of making that "touch of nature," or making the mantra, or expressing "what oft was thought," CLEARLY, publicly, consciously, to make that same unconscious awareness and desire appear up front in the public mind.

Aldrich: Mantra power, mantra power—Joyce! Right at the end of the *Portrait*, "I go to forge the uncreated conscience of my race," whatever, that's the same thing.

Ginsberg: Yeah.

Aldrich: To articulate that thing, and thereby to bring it into being.

Ginsberg: Well, yeah, see, it's *already* here, latently, in the unconscious, in other words it's like saying—it's just this way: there are two lovers sitting side by side, shy, and both of them want to make it, and they don't know how to break the ice. So, someone says, "Let's spend the night together!" So immediately, Ah! great sigh of relief, and they both understand and it's understood, let's do it. You know, we're gonna do it, you know, so. "I hereby declare the end of the war" simply sets up an example—that other people recognize their own feelings in, and brings that latent feeling up to the surface consciously, and then they can *act* on it. So it brings it into the . . . I forget what your phrase was just then—reality?

Aldrich: Articulation. Consciousness. Conscience.

Ginsberg: Well, you articulate your consciousness and then you can act it out. Once you're clear about what it is you want. Just sort of figuring out what you want and then acting it out.

In other words it isn't necessary for my word to like quote *overwhelm* or *convince,* unquote, anybody else, it's just necessary for me to place my word out there, not to overwhelm but to clarify other people's sane thought, or to make it conscious or to bring it to the surface of their minds, so they say: *Oh yeah! That's what I think too! Why didn't I say that before? I didn't think you were supposed to say that, I thought you were supposed to think about it maybe, but not say it, publicly . . .*

Aldrich: On another level—the same phenomenon of speech—I've done this dozens of times with novels, with poems, and that is I circle it all of a sudden on the page and say: Yeah, wow, I wish he hadn't said that, I wanted to say that!

Ginsberg: Yeah: What else—oh, I'm glad he said that, or I'm glad somebody said that. It's just, you know, the reaction: *Oh, groovy! somebody said it!* You know: *Gee, I thought that! Somebody finally laid it out!*

[Break.]

Ginsberg: So then: given, okay, given there's a whole area of new theory about how close you can get, on the page, to indicating or scoring, or notating, or whatever, the exact hesitancies, speedups, enjambments, syncopations . . .

Aldrich: Rhythms.

Ginsberg: Diffidences, emphases and tones of significant intention (musically) of the voice pronouncing the poems.

Well, first thing to realize is that (unless you're writing aloud, as on a tape machine), even if you're writing silently to yourself, there is *still a voice heard* in mind. So actually, it doesn't make too much difference if you compose aloud or on a page, and it doesn't make too much difference how you *score* voice detail minutiae, you don't have to score it too exactly—because it's like music, you score the main notes and then the interpreter can interpret it, with, you know, like, with his common sense. Like in music you *can* score things down exquisitely, closely, but you still have to say "andante" and everybody has to figure out what "andante" means to them, till there's a common practice. Well as people get more and more close to natural speech in poetry, there'll be a common practice and then an understanding rising, of how you read a broken line, on a page. See there wasn't a common practice before, because we were practicing a different kind of prosody. Till fifty years ago, esoterically; that is to say first Pound and Williams and a few people broke with that accentual practice fifty to sixty years ago and now all the poets have broken with the old practice and are writing out their own speech patterns nowadays, and so pretty soon there's a *common ear* and people understand automatically. Well, if you have a "but" all by itself on the page the guy is talking and then stops and says, "*but*" and then goes on.

Aldrich: Can you think of any guides for readers?

Ginsberg: Okay—guides for readers—Olson gave a whole lot of them, with the Projective Verse essay, about how the typewriter provides all sorts of new signs, like the slash mark, how on the typewriter you can go spurting on to the end of the page or you can just have one little independent hanging phrase—I've forgotten the—there was a series of little very practical pragmatic praxis tricks.

Aldrich: The one that clings most to my mind, and has for several years, is simply that you read any line-break as a break, you read any significant amount of white space as white space.

Ginsberg: Right.

Aldrich: Unless the poem is doing something avowedly different, for instance, painting a picture, in which case you don't pay much attention to the reading of the poem by white spacing.

Ginsberg: Yeah, well of course there's the end-stop, the breath-stop, as Creeley puts it, for his poems, like the end of a line is the end of a breath and you can, so Creeley says, *take a walk around the block and then come back and pronounce the next line.* Or for Olson it would be a hesitancy, or an *end* and then a beginning again. It's obvious what I do . . . it's the beginning of a thought, or a speech spurt, I put down at the left margin. Then any side thoughts, or qualifications of that, or extensions of that, I hang, indented, underneath that first marginalized statement. So in that sense, a little bit like, as I said before, diagramming a sentence grammatically. You diagram your thought, hanging it around on the page underneath the first thought.

Aldrich: And when you want to restart,

Ginsberg: Then you start again, like "Who" again—

Aldrich: Back at the left margin.

Ginsberg: So the *margin* provides the "Who," finally, provides the—what is the word you used?

Aldrich: Provides the anaphora.[38]

Ginsberg: The margin provides the anaphora.

Aldrich: Yeah! Wow, bingo, click!

Ginsberg: The anaphoric margin—so. That's one way. But Williams said, why is it that all poems have to start at the margin? What if they started at the end, or the other side? Or . . .

Aldrich: Well, that's also like asking, why do we not read boustrophedon,[39] and why don't we . . .

Ginsberg: No—but there are several thought gradations that don't need to start at the margin, that's what he was pointing out, and if you look at some of *Paterson* you'll find that's so. When you're waking up, and you emerge in the middle of a thought, then why begin *that* at the margin? You should begin that in the middle of the page—which I do sometimes, like—the only example in this book [*Planet News*] that I can think of offhand is the beginning of a poem called "Drowse Murmurs," which is literally drowse murmurs, it begins in the middle of a sentence, so it doesn't begin on the margin, it begins . . .

Aldrich: Does it begin in the middle of drowsiness?

Ginsberg: Literally, I wrote it when I was waking up from a drowse, in a bed in London, so it is that exactly. I begin at the margin in the sense that I begin the *dots* at the margin to create a space:

> . . . touch of vocal flattery
> exists where you wake us
> at dawn with happy sphinx

So it begins, not at the exact margin, it begins, I just start . . . and I might have, as well have, made a . . . made it come out further . . . Wonder what I, where, what else begins that way.

Aldrich: There's one where I noticed you broke up the word "electric," you cut it in half, in one of the poems, in *Airplane Dreams*. Here—the "New York to San Fran" poem again:

> A technicolor picture begins
>   on channel one—Elec
>   tronic Bee music.[40]

Ginsberg: Well, that's because—a technicolor picture begins on channel one; and then all of a sudden, they switch the elec-click to some kind of Stockhausen electronic music thing and it was to indicate a nonhuman vocal cord event—actually the picture on the screen was a great steel safe door crashing shut. The next line—

> The great steel safe door
>   crashes shut.
> The buzzing sciencefiction
>   lights & gauges ascend like

begin flashing, then you get this weird music, you know,

mmmmmmmmmmmmmmmmmmmmmmmmmmmmmmmmmmmmmmmmmmmm

So—electronic bee music; it was just sort of onomatopoeic, almost.

Aldrich: That's also witty.

Ginsberg: Yeah . . .

Aldrich: Go ahead—do you have something else?

Ginsberg: Yeah. Williams also suggested—where *I* began, actually, in that—was from one line of Williams that turned me on to realize his voice actually speaking and that speech reflected on the page—accurately—was at the end of a poem called "The Clouds." He has this fantastic passage about . . . the *imagination.* Forgotten how it goes, the imagination plunging through the clouds on a—he's talking about a loose imagination that doesn't have anything fixed, and is not working on anything real, just bullshitting, lunging on a moth, a butterfly, pismire, a . . .

He ends the poem there![41]

Ah—*a moth, a butterfly, a pismire, a . . .*

I heard him read it in the Museum of Modern Art, he just read it and read it ending with an impatient "uh"—a, a *nothing*, you know, there's no words for it.

Aldrich: Or anything.

Ginsberg: And he read it. And then he just waved his hand like that—"uh"—and then just silence.

Aldrich: Beautiful.

Ginsberg: And then went on to the next poem. And then I looked on the page and that's what was on the page, and I had never understood why it ended that way. I thought it was sort of like the mind drifting off—but it wasn't that, it was the mind coming to a point of irritation and annoyance so vague that it just went (shrug) pfft! and that was all.

So it depended on my actually hearing him vocalize that, to understand the exact tone, but that's because such a tone had never been . . .

Aldrich: Put on a page.

Ginsberg: . . . put on a page and written down in poetry before. That was the first time it was ever done, in a monologue poem. Maybe it might have been done in the theatre, but not in a monologue poem. I'm sure it's something that's been done in Shakespeare, or in a theatre or something, but it'd never been done as part of a poem. Or maybe Browning did it, maybe you could find some score in Browning, an instance where somebody got mad and shut up! —So that was the first thing I noticed, that he had—that it was ended with a whole line of dots.

Aldrich: Oh, I was hoping he'd just left the "a"—

Ginsberg: I think he has a whole line of dots after an "a" but I'm not sure—I'd have to look, see how he did it.

Then another trick he had was to put a dot, which is like a set thing, a period, not a period it was just a dot, not at the bottom of the line where the period is, but up in the middle, just a dot to indicate a break, either a break in the composition or a break in time or a break in thought.

Aldrich: He does that in, I think uh . . .

Ginsberg: In *Paterson* a lot.

Aldrich: He does it in *Pictures from Brueghel* too.

Ginsberg: Then there's another way he did—what's interesting is the interruptions, the interruptions of the mind. Mind interruptions, which is like the great problem since we're making a graph of mental operations, verbal forms—then the interruptions are of interest, are one of the key materials for scoring on the page. Where *do* you make a break, where you shift, where you jump—at least in Williams' way of doing it.

There's one in the poem called "For Eleanor and Bill Monahan,"[42] which when you read it does not seem to be an integral line, until you hear him read it on a Caedmon record: "What/ do they think they will attain/ by their ships/ that death has not/ already given/ them?"

Aldrich: That exact white space . . .

Ginsberg: Exact white space there. It's a real great thing to read the poem, and then hear Williams pronounce it. Do you know the record?

Aldrich: No.

Ginsberg: His record, *William Carlos Williams Reading His Poems*, a late Caedmon record[43] of *The Desert Music*, which I first heard when Creeley played it to me, and Williams is so much in his actual speaking-man reality on that, he trembles on the verge of tears occasionally. And every word he pronounces is exactly meaningful there, like somebody talking. And it's like the greatest of—his practice has come to complete perfection almost—his intention of practice all along has finally come to a conclusion—and technically, too, with a line like "What do they think they will attain/ by their ships/ that death has not/ already given/ them?" Then he says: "Their ships/ should be directed/ inward upon" and then he can't articulate it, he doesn't know exactly upon what the ships should be turned, but he knows they should be turned *inward*, and that's all he has to know, you know, as an old man and as a human being at this point in history. But he can lay that out as, that is what we need to know, I mean that's a problem we're facing so: "Their ships/ should be directed inward upon . But I/ am an old man. I/ have had enough."

Which is like a great dramatic fucking thing! and is always scored properly on the page. And then, "The female principle of the world/ is my appeal/ in the extremity/ to which I have come." And he goes into prayer: "*O clemens! O pia! O dolcis!/ Maria!*"

Aldrich: All of these devices I've been dreaming up and seeing in poems, and that you've been talking about—are essentially a romantic, expressionistic way of organizing a poem. You don't organize a poem along lines of a story that you have to tell, like an epic; you don't even organize a ballad type of poem along a narrative in which one stanza is one part of the story; you don't organize it logically like a sonnet; you don't even organize it logically like John Donne. It's not an intellectual logic or a narrative logic.

Ginsberg: I think it *is* an intellectual logic—because you're organizing it logically, to follow the precise forms of the movement of the mind. So I don't see it as romantic-expressionistic at all—I see it as absolutely logical scientific notation of event.

Kissam: Isn't it logical the way that montage is? I mean—

Ginsberg: Yeah, well montage is logical— montage was at first considered to be illogical, and irrational, or surrealism was first considered to be irrational, until everybody realized that what really was irrational was a rearrangement of the actuality of mind consciousness into syntactical forms which didn't have anything to do with what was going on in the head! So that finally the practical, pragmatic, common-sense form of notation of thought, was the surrealistic one, because that's the way the mind works.

So it may turn out that we've been undergoing centuries

of—this is what Blake was complaining about—of Newtonian thought. God save us from Newton's thought and somebody's—somebody else's—Bacon's funk. Or something.

Aldrich: Voltaire, Voltaire.

Ginsberg: What Blake was saying is that they were *unreal*, in the sense that it was just the creation of an imaginary universe and what could be more illogical? And what could be more logical than the actual clear demarcation and definition of the way the mind works?

Aldrich: Yeah. Um. I underrstand that. What I was thinking of is, for instance, "Ode to a Nightingale." It is not organized to tell a story, it's organized in such a way that you get Keats' thoughts as they come and as they are suggested and reflected in that bird—back and forth between his perception of that bird, there, and his own thinking about dying, and his own consciousness of everything that goes on. So the interplay, the tension that builds in the "Ode to a Nightingale" is expressionistic in the sense that it's not organized along a narrative line, nor a line in which you're trying to tell a logical sequence of events, as e.g. in Shakespeare's sonnets.

Ginsberg: Yeah.

Aldrich: Or even more, Petrarch's sonnets.

Ginsberg: Yeah.

Aldrich: Now we're moving; we've had this printed poem ever since—

Ginsberg: Since the invention of movable type, which is not very long. We've had the printed poem for a short period within 40,000 years of poetic history, now we've had the printed poem for approximately one one-hundredth of that time!

Aldrich: Yeah—who was the guy who first printed Chaucer?

Ginsberg: Caxton, er? Something like that, I don't remember.

Aldrich: Caxton, yeah.

Ginsberg: The older tradition, the most ancient tradition and . . . *the* tradition, the conservative tradition, the actual tradition, is oral.

The oral tradition has all of the mnemonic devices, and variations of rhythm and speech things . . . possible. The main structural guiding thing would be convenience in memorizing, I imagine, so that would be why alliterative repetition or rhythm or rhyme is used.

Aldrich: That's why the *Rig-Veda* comes down to us and that's why *Beowulf* comes down to us. Because those mnemonic devices were sufficient to allow people to remember them, generation to generation.

Ginsberg: It would be interesting to know what are the mnemonic devices of the Australian aborigines, who apparently have the largest and most complex system of oral tradition of any cultural group. See 'cause they don't have writing, at all.

Aldrich: Didn't know that.

Ginsberg: So the Australian aborigines are probably, in terms of the nonwritten culture, the most sophisticated. What they carry in their head; the most sophisticated memory'd linguistic group of any. In other words, apparently the Aborigines have fantastically long epics—and a dazzling aptitude for audiographic memory repetition of those epics. Like Homer—all of their culture, being oral, that means all of their creation myths, metaphysics, stories, narratives, histories—all of that is carried around in the head—and apparently they have an extremely extensive library in their head—because they think that way. We don't have to because we've got the crutch—written language is a mind crutch—we can put it down on a piece of paper so we don't have to remember anything. But they have to remember everything, so apparently they've specialized in not getting hung up on external things—the only possession that they have, for instance—their only tool—is a single purpose tool which also is used as a headrest—like it's some sort of wooden stick-cane-spoon, which they can sleep on, eat with, kill with, wash themselves with, count on.[44]

Aldrich: Brush their teeth with?

Ginsberg: Probably brush their teeth with. Now they reduced that all to a single multipurpose tool—no other possessions, no houses, practically—and so everything is in their consciousness. All other activity is in their consciousness. Like the whales, who are also probably in that situation, or the porpoises—like porpoises have a fantastic language, according to Gregory Bateson, mostly dealing with infinite gradations of interpersonal relations. Subtleties of interpersonal relations that we haven't conceived of—because that's all they've got, they don't have hands, machines, and they don't get hung up on building Empire State buildings—all of their attention is directed at each other.

Aldrich: No wonder John Lilly and people like that are really into whale communication!

Ginsberg: Yeah—Bateson was working with Lilly, and that was his conclusion.

Aldrich: Directions away from the printed poem. Right there [pointing at the Uher], you've got your direction away from the printed poem—in the tape recorder.

Ginsberg: Not really, it is the same thing—the tape recorder's not much different from writing in a notebook.

The reason I'm able to use a tape recorder so adequately, or the reason I adapted to it almost instantly, was that it was basically the same process as a notebook. Because I'm just doing the same thing in a notebook that I do on tape. At times a tape is more convenient, at times a notebook is more convenient. But I can shift back and forth. In fact I have poems which are begun on the tape recorder and the tape recorder ran down, battery ran down but I just continued in a notebook—and it's the same. The thing traveling west, north of Lincoln, Nebraska a year after the "Witchita Vortex Sutra."[45]

Aldrich: Okay, I'm trying to think of ways in which—

Ginsberg: The way beyond the printed page is music! Bob Dylan. That's the inevitable . . . well. The first way out is simply platform chanting, like William Jennings Bryan, or Vachel Lindsay or Dylan Thomas or myself or whoever makes it on the platform—the vocalization. The bardic thing. Platform bardic— Aah! [laughs to himself] Then next—at least in America at this point—it seems historically to have led to a revival of poetry as *song*.

To some extent Dylan was influenced by the whole wave of

poetry that went before and he got to thinking of himself as a poet, except a singing poet.

Aldrich: Sure—Woody Guthrie. Singing poet.

Ginsberg: Yeah. So song, which fits in with Pound's famous scheme you know, where he says the trouble with poetry is that it departs from song, and the trouble with song is that it departed from *dance*. In the *ABC of Reading*, or somewhere—*Guide to Kulchur?* Pound says that what happened historically was a big goof. Poetry began—the ictus (beat in the foot) of poetry originally was the Greek footfall as the chorus *chanted* and *danced*. And so the measure originally was literally the physical *stance* or *foot measure*. And that's what the *ictus / hit* is and that's what the measure was.[46]

Then, when poetry left that and got to be just chanting it lost some of the physical base—it got a little bit more disembodied. When it left the physical chanting and went to song it got slightly more disembodied, when it left song and got to speech it got slightly more disembodied, when it left speech and got to the printed page—and wasn't even spoken aloud, it became completely disembodied and that's the nineteenth-century vagueness of "dim vales of peace" and nothing means anything any more, words move no thing, it's totally abstract. So the next step was to bring words back to actual speech; then the next step after Pound modeling words from actual speech, and Williams' actual speech, is to bring it to—chanting is the next step— Which is what we did, chant—the next step was to bring it to song again, which is what Dylan did, and then the next step will be what Jagger and the others do, which is shamanistic dance-chant-body rhythm "I wanna go hooome, no satisfaction!" So what's happening in rock and roll, with all the body thing which is being laid on, and the dancing—or what the spades were doing, with all those funny little dances while they're singing (you know, a quartet singing words and then dancing) is actually a return cycle,[47] following Pound's original analysis, in a way.

So ultimately what you can expect is a naked, prophetic kid getting up, on a stage, chanting, in a trance state, language, and dancing his prophecies, all simultaneously in a state of ecstasy, which is, precisely, the return to the *original religious shamanistic prophetic priestly Bardic magic!*

NOTES

[1]"New York to San Fran," *Airplane Dreams: Compositions from Journals* (Toronto: Anansi, 1968), p. 11.

[2]*Airplane Dreams*, p. 22.

[3]Hart Crane: *The Complete Poems & Selected Letters & Prose*, ed. by Brom Weber (New York: Doubleday-Anchor, 1966), p. 116.

[4]"Television Was a Baby Crawling Toward That Deathchamber," *Planet News* (San Francisco: City Lights, 1968), pp. 15-32.

[5]*Planet News*, p. 15.

[6]*Planet News*, p. 29.

[7]*Planet News*, pp. 28-29.

[8]*Planet News*, pp. 29-30.

[9]*Planet News*, p. 30.

[10]See *Journals: Early Fifties Early Sixties*, ed. by Gordon Ball (New York: Grove Press, 1977), pp. 168-70.

[11]"Portland Coloseum," *Planet News*, pp. 102-103.

[12]Robert Creeley, *Contexts of Poetry: Interviews 1961-1971* (Bolinas, CA: Four Seasons Foundation, 1973), pp. 29-41.

[13]*Planet News*, pp. 110-32.

[14]*Planet News*, p. 127.

[15]Published as *The Fall of America, Poems of These States, 1965-1971* (San Francisco: City Lights, 1972).

[16]*Planet News*, pp. 123-24.

[17]*Planet News*, p. 30.

[18]*Ezra Pound at Spoleto* (New York: Applause Prod., Inc., SP411m, 1968).

[19]Ezra Pound, *Con Usura* [Canto XLV] (Scrittori Su Nastro II, Universita Degli Studia e Milano, EP 1V6001B, 1958).

[20]The section of the *Bhagavad-Gita* referred to is Chapter 10, sloka 35: see Radhakrishna edition p. 226.

[21]William Blake, "The Little Black Boy," in "Songs of Innocence," *The Portable Blake*, ed. by Alfred Kazin (New York: Viking, 1946), p. 86.

[22]William Blake, *Songs of Innocence and Experience*, tuned by Allen Ginsberg (N.Y.: MGM-Verve FTS-3083 [Side 1, Band 4], 1970).

[23]Charles Olson, "Projective Verse," in *Selected Writings*, ed. by Robert Creeley (New York: New Directions, 1966), p. 19:

> Let me put it baldly. The two halves are:
> the HEAD, by way of the EAR, to the SYLLABLE
> the HEART, by way of the BREATH, to the LINE

[24]Jack Kerouac, "The Art of Fiction XLI," *Paris Review*, no. 43, Summer 1968, pp. 60-105.

[25]"Projective Verse" was first published in *Poetry New York*, no. 3, 1950.

[26]Jack Kerouac, "Essentials of Spontaneous Prose," in *New American Story*, ed. by Donald Allen and Robert Creeley (New York: Grove Press, 1965), pp. 270-71.

[27]Published as *Empty Mirror* (New York: Totem/Corinth, 1961).

[28]Gary Snyder and Philip Whalen met William Carlos Williams when he visited Reed College in November 1950.

[29]*The Nassau Literary Magazine*, February 1964, p. 18.

[30]Rhythmic paradigm of "Lester Leaps In"—awkwardly remembered. —A.G.

[31]Allen Ginsberg, "Notes on Howl," *Allen Ginsberg Reads Howl and Other Poems*, Fantasy Record #7006 (1959).

[32]"Notes on Howl," reprinted in *The New American Poetry, 1945-1960*, ed. by Donald Allen (New York: Grove Press, 1960), pp. 414-18.

[33]"Sunflower Sutra," *Howl & Other Poems* (San Francisco: City Lights, 1956), pp. 28-30.

[34]*Kaddish and Other Poems* (San Francisco: City Lights, 1961), pp. 7-36.

[35]"Wichita Vortex Sutra," *Planet News*, p. 127.

[36]*Ibid.*

[37]Paul Carroll, *The Poem in Its Skin* (Chicago: Follet/Big Table, 1968), p. 101.

[38]Anaphora—(Greek, act of carrying back): repetition at the beginning of two or more successive clauses or verses especially for rhetorical or poetic effect. (Webster's Collegiate, 1963).

[39]Boustrophedon, writing as the cow turns: line 1 from left to right, line 2 from right to left, line 3 from left to right, etc.

[40]*Airplane Dreams*, p. 22.

[41]Williams Carlos Williams, *Collected Later Poems* (New York: New Directions, 1963), p. 128.

[42]William Carlos Williams, *Pictures from Brueghel* (New York: New Directions, 1962), pp. 85-86.

From "For Eleanor and Bill Monahan":

There are men
        who as they live
                fling caution to the
wind and women praise them
        and love them for it.
                Cruel as the claws of
a cat . . .

The moon which
        they have vulgarized recently
                is still
your planet
        as it was Dian's before
                you. What
do they think they will attain
        by their ships
                that death has not
already given
        them? Their ships
                should be directed
inward upon · But I
        am an old man. I
                have had enough.
The female principle of the world
        is my appeal
                in the extremity
to which I have come.
        O clemens! O pia! O dolcis!
                Maria!

[43]*William Carlos Williams Reading His Poems* (New York: Caedmon TC 1047, 1958).

[44]This piece of mythical anthropologic data is adapted after gossip heard from Harry Smith's lips, possibly a hippie bull-roarer (churinga) reinvented in Western eternal dream time. See A. P. Elkin, *The Australian Aborigines* (New York: Doubleday-Anchor, 1964), pp. 185-89. —A.G.

[45]Allen Ginsberg, "Returning North of Vortex," *Planet News*, pp. 64-68.

[46]Ictus means struck, as with a lance (or foot?)—also remember "a foot is to kick with"—Charles Olson

[47]"As the old Egyptian devotee sings, dances and perhaps plays some musical instrument before his God . . ."—Sydney Lanier, *Science of English Verse* (New York: Scribner's, 1920), p. 265.

THE NEW CONSCIOUSNESS

["This conversation was recorded in Manhattan on a hot, sultry, electric night of August 1972 in Allen Ginsberg's small apartment on the Lower East Side. The windows were open and on the tape one can hear background noises of children laughing, dogs barking and, at frequent intervals, the wailing of police cars. Allen was just back from the Miami Republican convention in the course of which he had spent 3 days in jail with some Yippies and Zippies. He seemed a little tired, having caught a cold, and spoke in a deep, slightly hoarse voice. But he was very courteous and, though I was meeting him for the first time, willing to offer as much help and information as he could. I was struck and charmed to see how thoroughly and scrupulously he answered any question. He is a long-winded talker, picking his words carefully, I would say almost with *delectation,* as if they were ripe cherries, and associating them in long sentences without losing the thread of his exposition. Originally I had come to ask a few factual questions about Kerouac but our conversation expanded and when I left late in the night I realized I had just been hearing a fairly detailed chronicle of the whole poetic movement he had been associated with since the 40s. From the outset he asked me who, 'among our group,' I had already visited, and as I had recently met Kenneth Rexroth on the West Coast, we started speaking of his appearance in *The Dharma Bums* under the pseudonym of Rheinhold Cacoethes."— Yves Le Pellec. The interview was published in the "Beat Generation" issue of *Entretiens,* No. 34, 1975.]

Allen Ginsberg: Cacoethes in English means bad habit, I think.

Yves Le Pellec: Yes, and I found a short note Jack [Kerouac] sent to Larry Ferlinghetti saying Rexroth had the habit of scribbling all the time, that he was an "inveterate scribbler."

Ginsberg: Well, Rexroth was an older person, so he wasn't among the younger comrades and he had at the time a great deal of pride built up over many years of literary isolation. His reaction to Kerouac was that of an elder who was very often surprised, shocked and sometimes irritated by what he interpreted to be bad manners, which were on occasion bad manners like a few times when Jack was drunk in his house—not really bad manners but sick manners—but Rexroth went through many modifications of his judgment. His judgment is generally benevolent and friendly now but at one time he thought Kerouac was a horrible writer and a very bad poet and he wrote a devastating attack on Kerouac in *The New York Times* on the appearance of the . . .

Le Pellec: *Mexico City Blues?*

Ginsberg: *Mexico City Blues*, a very stupid review. *Mexico City Blues* is a great classic, I think, I mean it taught me poetics, and it taught Michael McClure a great deal, and is one of the great presentations of Buddhism in American terms. It has many many virtues, it's a completely original book, with a self-invented poetics in it, it has a marvelous ear and marvelous rhythms. So that's a work of genius, an extended work of genius, 242 linked poems like a Shakespearean sonnet sequence, it's just a remarkable monolithic work of jazzing up the American language, as Céline said about Henri Barbusse's prose. He said he liked Barbusse because he jazzed up the language.

Le Pellec: But Rexroth did a lot to help at the beginning: his first articles, the "San Francisco Letter" [in *Evergreen Review*, No. 2, 1957] . . .

Ginsberg: Yes, a great deal, a great deal. His first appreciations were accurate and very sympathetic and good-hearted. The difficulty came after our work was out in public and was very heavily attacked, particularly Kerouac's, by a sort of literary establishment that were pleased with the status quo in America, many of whom actually were unconsciously involved with the CIA thru the Congress for Cultural Freedom, which published *Encounter*, a "front" and a magazine which was being funded by the CIA. Kerouac's completely unofficial version of America was very displeasing to them and their immediate reaction was that it was some sort of cult of violence, exhibitionism, rather than realizing it was a sincere heart-speech, a pacifistic heart-speech really. So these attacks delayed the acceptance of both the mode of speech, that is the style of speech and the physiology, the rhythms of such speech, as well as the general ideas and the intellectual background, which was gnostic rather than rationalistic. This stunted the development of American culture for a long time. So that when the style, the stylistic attributes, were picked up by later generations—that is to say spontaneous speech, the use of drugs on the side, marijuana and psychedelics, the preoccupation with American Indians, the second religiousness that Kerouac spoke of (the phrase being Spengler's), the interest in black music or the sense of a Fellaheen subterranean underground nonofficial existence—the intellectual background and the rationalization for it, the literary background for it, was not transmitted rapidly enough. The intellectuals said that it came out of no tradition, they were not smart enough or learned enough to know the tradition, or sensitive enough to understand it. The tradition for instance in Kerouac is the black blues. It wasn't until the 60s—'62 or'63—with Amiri Baraka (LeRoi Jones) leading an attack on white culture and presenting the black culture and black blues as a major art form in America, that it got to be accepted as a major art form with the intellectual distinction that it has. Well, Kerouac was dealing with those forms earlier but none of the academic critics that attacked him in the 50s had any idea of the body of poetics that you find here—[showing a book] *The Blues Line* by Eric Sackheim, 1969—the body of poetics which Kerouac was drawing on for his *Mexico City Blues*. Most of his critics had no idea of this as literature, the true literature in America, and it was. Also in *Mexico City Blues* or in other writings of '53, '54, '55, Kerouac wrote with great sophistication on Buddhism and the basic tenets of Buddhism being that existence is Dukha, or suffering—but most of his critics were not familiar with that. So when he cited, say, the *Prajnaparamita Sutra* or *Diamond Sutra* or *Lankavatara Sutra*, probably many of his critics thought he was talking gibberish, without realizing he was citing very ancient and honorable texts. So that Kerouac was met with a barrage of enormous stupidity both in America and France, as a reaction to his presentation and transmission of wisdom texts. So when Rexroth—who was the older critic who took everybody seriously, read all the works and knew about Eastern thought—read *Mexico City Blues* so improperly and thought that it was some childish scatological babblings, it was a great blow to the advancement of the general culture in America, it just killed maybe ten years' time.

Le Pellec: Some people have discussed Kerouac's attitude towards jazz. I think he has been reproached for having a "white man's" attitude, liking musicians like George Shearing for instance rather than more important musicians, and not being really into the soul of blues.

Ginsberg: Well, I think that's a very superficial *examen de texte.* If you look at Kerouac's texts, all of them, his approach was primarily oriented to Charlie Parker. He didn't *write* about Charlie Parker, he *participated* in those situations; he was in Harlem, at Minton's when Parker and Thelonious Monk and Dizzie Gillespie were there *playing,* back in the early 40s. He was there on the spot, he was there participating in some of the first recordings made there, including recordings of Charlie Christian. I remember that from 1944 he was introducing me to sound, to Parker. That was his main interest. Then he was interested in the later developments. By the 50s the great bop revolution had reached its peak and it was time for another wave, and there was another wave of exfoliation, and spreading out and development of the rhythmic changes that had been taking place in bop, and a passing of these new musical techniques onto the white culture. People like Lennie Tristano and George Shearing picked them up and so Kerouac noted that and wrote about that. He followed it closely, like a baseball player interested in the progress of the teams throughout the season and who all the players were. So he wrote about the American jazz milieu. Very early, at a time when very few people were even paying attention to this music, Kerouac made a little record with Zoot Sims and Al Cohn—do you know that recording of haiku?[1] That was the only recording of jazz and poetry that was original and recorded in the studio spontaneously. See, all the rest was sort of like background music, or prepared music or music that had nothing to do really with the poetry. Kerouac would pronounce a little haiku like "The bottom of my shoes are wet, from walking in the rain" and Al Cohn or Zoot Sims would take the rhythmic thing [sings] "ta ba da ba ta ta, ta ta, ta da da ta ta ta," a little haiku of music, then Kerouac would go, "In my medicine cabinet the winter fly has died of old age," then Al Cohn would go "Ta Ra ta ta da ta ta, ta ra ta ta, ta ra da da da." So they would make rhythmic structures mirroring each other. Kerouac actually *was* a musician, or good enough to work with musicians. He had a sophistication, a prosody, a musical ear much greater than any of his critics were capable of . . . So I think that the criticism of his interest in the younger white musicians is out of the context of the development of jazz in America. For at that time a great deal of the notoriety and energy of the original bop changes went over to Shearing, Tristano, Lee Konitz and others. The next great round of creation came in the late 50s with the public emergence, not onto the commercial scene but onto the social scene in New York, of Ornette Coleman, Don Cherry, Cecil Taylor, Albert Ayler . . . Kerouac was then very much on the scene also for it was associated with his mood at the time. One of the people that he influenced a great deal, both in his appreciation of jazz and his appreciation of black culture, was LeRoi Jones. Around 1958 Jones became a sort of intellectual arbiter and energy setter in New York City. Just about a few blocks from here he had a big house, gave parties in his floor-thru and had his magazine *Yūgen*. Kerouac was still in the city and sociable and saw Jones quite a bit, so he was still around when the next great phase of black music arrived. Beyond all that, Kerouac's ultimate forte was with alcoholic street musicians, the real blues, the ultimate blues of people that don't even have an instrument but just stand in the doorway and say [sings]:

> I'm standing in the doorway
> Got no place to go
> Standing in the doorway
> Got no place to go
> Jack Kerouac gave me fifty cents
> And I'll go out and blow.

Kerouac could improvise blues, which is *the* tradition, the great classic tradition. In that sense he was himself black. Partly what destroyed him also was the alcoholic bum he was, the bum of the Third Street in San Francisco or Bowery here. He wrote *Third Street Blues* and *Bowery Blues* which I don't think have been completely published.

Le Pellec: Aren't they in *Scattered Poems?*

Ginsberg: Fragments of them. So Kerouac spent a lot of time drinking in doorways with blues singers and was very close to the actuality of blues, universal blues, neither black nor white. I think that the sort of criticism that's proposed here is . . . "distant folly." You may not like Shearing but I think he *is* a good musician. The contribution Shearing made, he made then, that is to say in the late 40s, 22 years ago. We are talking about an era when musicians like Shearing, Konitz, Tristano were beginning to, like, make a scene of their own, which I don't think was an important scene, historically, and possibly Kerouac in his enthusiasm overpraised them but I think the time capsule that he gives is perfect, perfect for that time.

Le Pellec: Could we speak of the early days in New York, the mid 40s, when you were at Columbia. From what I've read and heard I found that many of Kerouac's friends considered him as *the* intellectual, almost the scholar. Neal, for instance, regarded him as a man who had a university culture. Yet he had spent only one or two years at Columbia?

Ginsberg: And then in '49 he went to the New School for Social Research. He had already written *The Town and the City.* By his standards that was a very great piece of prose, traditional prose, but it was like the last possible gasp of such orchestral *Bildungsroman* prose, as in Thomas Wolfe. It was a great contribution to that actually. It's still a very valuable book and there are great prose passages in it. I think the description of Times Square is prophetic. It leads on to the whole hippy movement twenty years later.

Kerouac was always sort of an exile in the university community. He was a football player but when he quit I think the football bureaucracy got mad at him and took away his scholarship and he was not able to pay for his housing there. He was very brilliant in class, he got good marks from Mark Van Doren, who was a Shakespeare scholar and a poet.

Le Pellec: He was your professor too?

Ginsberg: I had him for one term, in fact I had six or seven professors each term. The one professor who had good relations with me and Jack and who respected Jack's prose then, the only one, was a man named Raymond Weaver. He was the first biographer of Melville and the discoverer of the manuscript of *Billy Budd.* He wrote a book called *Herman Melville, Mariner and Mystic.* At Columbia he was a considerable intellectual presence, like an old-fashioned scholar and at the same time a very modern soulful intellectual. He was sort of mystic, gnostic, he had lived in Japan and used some Zen for teaching. So Kerouac had written a manuscript the name of which I don't remember . . . It was before *The Town and the City* . . .

Le Pellec: Wasn't it "The Sea is My Brother"?

Ginsberg: I think it's in between, it was another little thing, a little romance about angels coming down fire escapes [laughs]. He took it to Weaver and Weaver recommended that Jack read the Egyptian Gnostics, Jacob Boehme, Blake, *The Egyptian Book of the Dead,* perhaps *The Tibetan Book of the Dead* and I think some Zen classics. So Weaver perceived immediately the magical aspect of Kerouac's character and his mystical potential. Everybody else around that scene was very materialistic in the sense of "If you write a story it should have a middle, a beginning, and an end, and you shouldn't have too many fancy words because you know it's not in the tradition of realism that might grow out of the older proletarian novel and make sense in the new America facing the post-war future . . . " Everybody was writing sort of rationalistic discourses putting down the communists and very heavily political in a very negative way, in a very status quo way, and most of them were writing about manners, and good manners were Henry James and Jane Austin in those days. Whereas Kerouac was writing about the descent of angels in workman's overalls, which was basically the really great American tradition from Thoreau through Whitman . . .

Le Pellec: Was Whitman taught at Columbia?

Ginsberg: He was taught but he was much insulted. I remember, around the time of the writing of *On the Road,* a young favored instructor at Columbia College told me that Whitman was not a serious writer because he had no discipline and William Carlos Williams was an awkward provincial, no craft, and Shelley was a sort of silly fool! So there was no genuine professional poetics taught at Columbia, there was a complete obliteration and amnesia of the entire great mind of gnostic western philosophy or Hindu Buddhist eastern philosophy, no acceptance or conception of a possibility of a cosmic consciousness as a day to day experience or motivation or even once in a lifetime experience. It was all considered as some sort of cranky pathology. So Whitman was put down as "a negativist crude yea-sayer who probably had a frustrated homosexual libido and so was generalizing his pathology into oceanic consciousness of a morbid nature which had nothing to do with the real task of real men in a real world surrounded by dangerous communist enemies" [laughs] or something like that . . .

Le Pellec: The same things were said about you and Jack in the first reviews you got. The term "narcissistic" recurs very often.

Ginsberg: Sure, it's just typical of the Pentagon to call anybody that criticizes their policy narcissistic and unrealistic. You know, these people are depending on sixty billion dollars a year, that's a lot of heavy metal and appears real to them! And anybody who thinks that their heavy metal is the by-product of a mass hallucination would be considered mad by War Secretary Laird. The crucial point, I think, is that the original criticism of the texts that came out—McClure's, Snyder's, my own, Kerouac's—was based on a very narrow view of human nature, a definitely prepsychedelic experience of human nature, at a time when there was a definite shrinkage of sensitization, of sensory experience, and a definite mechanical disorder of mentality that led to the cold war and to the present genocidal ecocidal mass air-war in Indochina. The desensitization had begun, the compartmentalization of mind and heart, the cutting off of the head from the rest of the body, the robotization of mentality that could lead Harvard and Columbia intellectuals like Kissinger and Schlesinger, all those supposedly realistic, mature, ripeminded academics to pursue a 1984-style cybernetic warfare with all the moral rationalizations of self-righteous self-interest that you found in France when you had people asserting all sorts of moral *principes* to justify the war in Indochina or the war in Algeria . . . Which by hindsight are now considered to have been madness and cruelty and in fact criminality. At the same time we were being attacked by the university academic intellectuals because we were opening up an area of another consciousness, a planetary ecological consciousness, in a sense. Consciousness within the academy was narrowing down, becoming more anxious and rigid,[2] and it was the initiation of the cold war theoretics for them, the beginning of that grand international paranoia.

Le Pellec: But did you have the feeling that you were starting something, that a "new generation" was appearing? This spiritual awakening, which is obvious today, did you feel it just after the second World War?

Ginsberg: Not instantly, no. Actually the first perceptions that we were having, the first perceptions that we were separate from the official vision of history and reality, began around '45, '46, '47. We realized that there was a difference between the way we talked—Jack, Burroughs, myself, as comrades among ourselves in order to get information and give each other our best stories, just like between Neal and Jack, in order to share experience and find our ultimate heart or vision—and what we heard on the radio if any president or congressman or even literary person began talking officialese. The air was filled with pompous personages orating and not saying anything spontaneous or real from their own minds, they were only talking stereotypes. I remember Burroughs saying during one presidential campaign, I think when Truman was running for president, that if an elephant had walked up in front of all those candidates in the middle of a speech and shat on the ground and walked away, the candidate would have ignored it. Consciousness wasn't present there on the occasion when they were talking, consciousness was an abstract, theoretical state. A theoretical nation, the actual nation was not there. Which is basically the same thing that Ezra Pound and William Carlos Williams and Sherwood Anderson had been saying all along. So we saw the difference between our own speech, our own company, and the national company full of Ionescoesque hallucinations of language.

Then we began running into people on Times Square, Huncke, whom Kerouac describes already in '48, '49 in *The Town and the City*. Huncke was addicted to morphine, and in observing him we saw the difference between authoritarian law as imposed on Huncke's suffering as a sick junkie and what we saw in person: he was just sick and needed help and there was no reason why he shouldn't get his maintenance therapy, as it is called now, maintenance supply of drugs from a doctor. Huncke told us that the narcotics police themselves were peddling dope under the table just as in those very days General Raoul Salan and the entire

French intelligence in Indochina were organizing the dope trade for their own benefits or for their own paramilitary fundings—I've just been reading a book that goes over all that, *The Politics of Heroin in Southeast Asia*[3]—and all that was presented in France as some sort of higher morality [laughs].

Le Pellec: Heroic defense!

Ginsberg: Yes! So we saw that the police were making big moralistic speeches to the New York *Daily News* appealing to the most lower guttersnipe emotions accusing people of being dope fiends. Our friend Huncke was being called a Fiend! A new category of human being, namely the "human Fiend," had been created by the police at the same time as the police themselves were peddling dope and being brutal and violating the law and creating a police bureaucracy in this area. And the newspapers and *Time* magazine, *The New York Times, The Daily News* were of no help at all, it was all the police-bureaucracy line. So we realized there was simply a separation between our thought and public thought, between private consciousness and public consciousness. But Whitman all along had said that private consciousness *is* public consciousness, that the State doesn't exist *(as a living Person)*, only people exist through their own private consciousness. So we realized that we were in the midst of a vast American hallucination, that a hallucinatory public consciousness was being constructed in the air waves and television and radio and newspapers, even in literature. By hindsight we saw that part of that consciousness was being paid for by the CIA to the extent that they invaded the literary field, and the students' world later on with the National Students Association suborned and paid for by the CIA. But we didn't know all this in political terms, all we knew was that like we were making sense to each other, you know, talking from heart to heart, and that everybody else around us was talking like some kind of strange lunar robots in business suits. Everybody sounded like the police in some funny way, even the professors at the university. I remember in 1946, as early as that, I was considered unsavory on the campus. My deportment was proper and I was editing the campus newspaper, but I had a beard, I didn't shave every day, I shaved every five days, and I had very little money so I walked around in secondhand clothes and I had a somewhat chaplinesque look. And Kerouac was literally *banned* from physical presence on the campus because he quit the football team and had strange Dostoyevskian friends! It takes a Russian police state to conceive of such a stupid social situation. Because we all knew everybody, it was a small campus, four hundred students, and everybody knew everybody. And you banned somebody who was a writer, a poet! So, I remember, Kerouac came and stayed with me one night in 1946. He had spent the evening with Burroughs talking, Burroughs had warned him against his mother, he thought Kerouac would never be able to get away from her if he didn't make a break, and Jack was all disturbed so he came to my room in the residence hall, Livingston Hall I think, and said "I have been talking to Burroughs and he said the most interesting thing," so we started talking about that. I had written a long poem modeled on Rimbaud's "Bateau Ivre" and the Baudelaire voyage theme, it was called "Le Dernier Voyage," a very stupid poem, fifteen pages of rhymed couplets or something, and I read it to him. Then we went to bed, in the same bed, in underwear; at the time I was a virgin though I was in love with Kerouac, but I was very afraid to touch him . . .

Le Pellec: And what about him?

Ginsberg: Well, let me finish the story. So we slept very peacefully. But I had written on the windowpane, which was very dirty, like this window out here [rubbing dust off the windowpane] lot of dust here, "Butler has no balls"—Butler was the president of the University—and "Fuck the Jews" and drawn a skull and crossbones, thinking that the chambermaid would look at it and wash it off and clean the window. But instead she looked at it and reported it to the dean. So about eight in the morning the assistant dean of the student faculty relations burst into the room and saw me and Kerouac in bed. Now it turned out this man was formerly the football coach that Kerouac had worked with. So naturally the football coach assumed the worst. And Kerouac saw the situation and did something very characteristic of him: he jumped out of bed, ran into the next room, jumped into my roommate's bed, pulled the covers over his head and went back to sleep [laughs] and left me to face the situation. The assistant dean said, "Wipe that off the window," so I wiped it off the window, and when I went downstairs after about an hour I found a note in my box charging me 2 dollars and 35 cents for having an unauthorized visitor overnight and a note saying the dean of the college wanted to see me. So I went to see Dean McKnight an hour later. I sat down in his office and he looked at me very seriously and said: "Mr. Ginsberg, I hope you understand the enormity of what you have done." These were his opening words. Burroughs had just given us *Voyage au Bout de la Nuit.* Do you remember that scene when Céline is in the middle of the battlefield and realizes he is in a place surrounded by dangerous madmen? So I looked at the dean and remembered that phrase and thought "Watch out, he's a dangerous madman" [laughs]. The "*enormity*"*!* The word itself is incredible! So I said, "Yes I do, sir I do!" cringing and crawling, "I do," thinking 'what can I do to get out of this situation, how can I apologize?" The dean was mad and Columbia College was mad! Well, what I am trying to point out is the difference between the private consciousness that we had and the official public consciousness. The private consciousness was the camaraderie and common sense of talking very late at night showing poems, sleeping, having the personal subjective relations we had, the public sense was "Mr. Ginsberg, I hope you realize the enormity of what you have done!" I mean, to have banned Kerouac from the campus to begin with was an act of such great hysteria and stupidity and desensitivity and, I think, so unacademic! I mean, imagine Socrates trying to ban Alcibiades from conversation! It just wasn't proper, it just wasn't classical. And those people were posing as the inheritors of tradition and the guardians of learning and wisdom. In fact just at that point they were putting themselves in the service of the military and were building an atom bomb, secretly making the biggest political decision of the century without consulting the democratic populace, and by later examination one saw that the entire university had been turned over to capitalist vocational training.

Le Pellec: Did this awareness lead you to a political expression?

Ginsberg: I personally, and I think everybody around, immediately questioned the whole structure of Law and immediately apprehended the basic principles of philosophical anarchism. Kerouac had been a communist already, I even think he had been a member of the party. As a member of the National Maritime Union, before it had been taken over by right wing types and the CIA so to speak and the government—he was very overtly communistic for several years, from '39 to'41, '42.

Le Pellec: I didn't know that. I'm surprised. From what he wrote I would never have imagined him as a Marxist! And he had read Marx?

Ginsberg: Certainly, sure, Kerouac was very learned, you know, he was always very learned. I don't think he read it with any formal scholarship but I'm sure he read in and out of *Das Kapital* and read through *The Communist Manifesto* and maybe a few other things and he read the *Daily Worker*. It was not a phase that lasted very long, it was only two or three years. When was he born, in 1924?

Le Pellec: 1922.

Ginsberg: Well, it was 1940, '41 when he was a communist. He was 19, 20 years old, he was still like a young vigorous seaman. It's proper. Like any young man now. Just normal, quite normal. I think he got to dislike communist ideology later on because the Marxists' reception of his prose, my poetry, and Burroughs' prose was very stupid at first. I think the Marxists in general now feel that we were some sort of helpful, hopeful, useful, pre-revolutionary something, they've fitted us in somehow. But at the time there was a large attack by the left against the idea of revolution of consciousness, sexual revolution particularly, and psychedelic revolution involving chemicals and dope, even involving marijuana which is after all an old folk culture tribal totem. You would have thought they were smarter than that but they had very little anthropological training. There were two aspects that Kerouac objected to. First the tendency among the Marxists to deplore our bohemianism as some sort of petit bourgeois angelism, archangelistic tendencies, and to deny the existence of God, to deny the existence of the great empty universal consciousness. And also the left attempted to make the cultural revolution we were involved in, which was a purely personal thing, into a lesser political, mere revolt against the temporary politicians, and to lead the energy away from a transformation of consciousness to the materialistic level of political rationalism. But the Marxist rational interpretation of the psychological situation we saw in America was not sufficiently understanding, delicate, tender, to really apprehend the full evil of American society as far as its psychic effects on ourselves and, say, Dean McKnight were concerned. It was too linear, as they say now, an interpretation of the economic causation of the mass stupidity. Around 1948 we began having definite visionary experiences. We had been reading Rimbaud by the time, his letter to Georges Izambard about *"un long, immense et raisonné dérèglement de tous les sens."* Under the influence of Burroughs we already had had the experience of some of the opiates, on and off, and by 1952 we already had had the experience of peyotl partly as a result of translations of Artaud's *Voyage au Pays des Tarahumaras,* which appeared in *Transition* magazine in the 40s, and Huxley's *Doors of Perception.* Some of Kerouac's writings of '52, particularly his *Visions of Cody,* are some of the most brilliant texts written about the psychedelic experience, especially the description of him and Neal on peyotl. So I am talking about the development of a new consciousness, as they say now. I think the phrase is used in *The Greening of America* . . .

Le Pellec: Yes it is and I think Huxley already spoke of "expanding consciousness" in *The Doors of Perception.*

Ginsberg: In fact the phrase "New Consciousness" was already being used way back in the 50s. I think there was a little interview essay[4] with Burroughs and Corso and myself which uses the phrase with capital letters too . . . As it proved, in America, it was necessary to go through a long period of change of consciousness before people could be liberated from the hypnotic hallucination that they'd been locked in. It would have been premature to speak in political terms in those times. In fact we were definitely thinking in *non*-political terms, apolitical terms. The first necessity was to get back to Person, from public to person. Before determining a new public, you had to find out who you are, who is your person. Which meant finding out different modalities of consciousness, different modalities of sexuality, different approaches to basic identity, examination of the nature of consciousness itself finally—on a very serious level, meaning not only psychoanalysis and drugs but also meditation and ascetic experience, isolation and solitary experience, and shabda yoga and jazz and sexual exploration. And recovery of natural tongue, of speech forms that are real rather than literary forms, and recovery of body movement and song and dance, in those days catalyzed primarily by rhythm and blues, the precursor of rock 'n' roll. Like Neal and Jack driving around listening to black rhythm and blues.

Le Pellec: But later on you move towards a more "political" consciousness, in "Wichita Vortex Sutra" for instance.

Ginsberg: Yes, that's in the mid 60s.

Le Pellec: Whereas Jack sort of went away from it.

Ginsberg: Yes and no. There's a lot of rot on this. For one thing, it wasn't so much that I evolved as that there were finally enough people conscious to make a group, not just a few—ten, twenty people corresponding. We didn't have a post-Beatles mass, a whole generation of longhaired kids who had the experience of a second religiousness and of the recovery of their own body and of a sexual revolution. Then you can begin thinking how do we get together and how do we change things? What do we want and what do we formulate? What do we really want with America? What percent of the American energy supply does the aluminum industry take? Actually one third. And the Pentagon? Actually forty per cent. Now we can have actual research and it can be disseminated. So it was not possible really to be political until you had enough people to make a new nation. Also by that time Kerouac had suffered so much attack and abuse from all sides, left and right, particularly left in terms of the venomousness of it, and had become so entangled in personal problems with his mother and most of all had become so ill physically with alcoholism that he was not in a position to go out in the world very much. From 1960 on, every move he made outside of his home was dangerous for him because he would always drink himself so ill and get in trouble, people beating him up actually, left-wing literary critics beating him up [laughs]. Once he came drunk into a bar saying "I'm Jack Kerouac," and some radical goon, from the longshoremen's union, I think, beat his head on the pavement. It wasn't political quite, it was just some sort of macho ego thing. And Kerouac was very open, totally helpless. Then there was the tendency to vulgarize the renaissant spirituality of what he had proposed. One built-in stereotype which still exists and is poisoning the left here insists on "hatred" as a "revolutionary weapon," an old-fashioned pre-psychedelic nineteenth-century hatred, father and mother hatred actually, which was contrary to his nature as it is contrary to mine. This hatred is at the root of most radical consciousness in America as we saw in the last four years when the entire left went into a completely masturbatory period of social violence, calling everybody pigs, with self-righteousness and self-isolation which finally led to the election of Nixon. That gross element in the left repelled Kerouac, who felt that it was a betrayal of what he had prophesied. He prophesied a spiritual angelic generation that would ultimately take over with long hair and exquisite manners, you know, "wise as serpents and harmless as doves." Instead they were, like, greedy as pigs and harmful as dogs. It's still a problem, the left being poisoned by its own anger. Also his thing was very wise in that he was basically himself a populist redneck and his mother was like a French Canadian peasant, narrow-minded, selfish, naive, hard-hearted, family-oriented lady. She wanted to keep Jack to herself and needed Jack, and he was tied up with her in the sense that he said he didn't want to throw her to the "Dogs of Eternity," as he thought I had done, putting my mother in a mental hospital. So he felt bound to take care of her and, having to live with her, he had to put up with her opinions. In that sense Jack was always an "Americanist," always interested in American archetypes and his mother was like a George Wallace archetype so to speak. Like Céline, like Dostoevsky in old age, like Pound in some respect, like any Tolstoy anywhere, he had an odd cranky appreciation for right-wing archetypes that most left-wing writers are not subtle enough to appreciate. And so in a sense he fulfilled an interesting role there in poetizing that type. Harmless I would say, because it served to curb violent left excesses in myself and in other people. I mean, I always had Kerouac in mind when I got on a peace march and I always made sure it was like really straight, pure, surrealist, lamblike, non-violent, magical, mantric, spiritual politics rather than just marching up and down the street screaming hatred at the president. In a funny way he didn't have a position, he was just himself, his own character, reacting. He was against the war actually, in a redneck way. On a TV program with pro-war-scholar William F. Buckley, Jr., in 1968, he said of the South-Vietnamese politicians "All those guys, all they're trying to do is steal our jeeps." That's a very archetypal proposition and it's really true. He put the whole thing in a very intelligent way that could be universally understood, unlike New York dialectical doubletalk.

Le Pellec: Well, you could hear that sort of thing in any Café du Commerce in Bretagne.

Ginsberg: Yea. If you read his essays like *The Lonesome Traveler* they were really attacks on the police state. Always. The whole thrust of his work was towards individualism and freedom, the only thing is he very definitely took a stand on communist brainwashing. He designated it with the name of "Arapatienz," I don't know what his source was, in the encyclopedia I think, from the name of the Russian who invented mind-conditioning. That he felt was the great evil, which he ascribed to Russian communism as well as to the American *Time-Life* network. So his preoccupation was with individualism. Later he never got into a communal effort, possibly that was because there was no commune sufficiently mature and sweet to be able to take care of him and his mother. And above all there was the problem of his physical illness. When he died his body was in a terrible condition: he had a broken arm, a hernia in his belly-button area that he refused to have fixed, and apparently his liver was gone. I believe it was the night he finished the last chapter of *Pic*, his last novel, that he had the hemorrhage.

Le Pellec: He had started *Pic* in '51, '52, hadn't he?

Ginsberg: I don't remember. It's just a little thing that he did long ago. This is just the last chapter. Actually there is another last chapter that he didn't add, when Pic meets Dean Moriarty on his hitchhiking North. He wrote that chapter but I think his mother or his wife didn't like it. When that suppressed chapter is published ultimately, you'll see it's all tied back to the *On the Road* themes.

Le Pellec: Yea, and the episode of the Ghost of the Susquehanna recurs in *Pic*. Speaking of that period, I found a letter from you to Neal saying you didn't like Jack's new style when he started writing *On the Road*. And John Clellon Holmes also says in a letter of that time that he thought Jack was on the wrong way.

Ginsberg: I changed my mind very soon after that. It was a sort of superficial egotism on my part not to understand what he was doing. I was just a stupid kid. What did the letter say, I don't remember, that his new writing was all crazy or something?

Le Pellec: Yes and that it could be interesting only for somebody that had been blowing Jack for years [laughs].

Ginsberg: Oh, what a stupid thing to say! You know, I was very naive, he taught me everything I knew about writing. It took a long time, a couple of years I think, for me to appreciate his ability there and even a longer time for me to begin practicing in spontaneous composition. But my stupidity about his prose couldn't have lasted too long because pretty soon after I was running around New York with his manuscript trying to get people to publish it. At that time I was still writing very laborious square rhymed verse and revising, revising and revising. He was on my neck to improvise more and not to get hung up but I *resisted* that for a long, long time. All my conceptions of literature, everything I was taught at Columbia, would fall down if I followed him on that scary road! So it took me a long time to realize the enormous amount of freedom and intuition that he was opening up in composition.

Le Pellec: Was it with "Green Auto?"

Ginsberg: No that was revised but I was getting close. Actually it wasn't till I went out to his house, when he was living in Northport I believe, so this was '53, '54 really . . . I sat down at his typewriter and just typed what was in my head and came up with a funny poem about the Statue of Liberty that was about three pages, a very sloppy poem and I never published it because it was inferior. But he looked at it and pointed out all the interesting images and he said, "See, you can do it too." It was just that I was afraid to try, afraid to throw myself out into the sea of language, afraid to swim.

Le Pellec: In a June '53 letter to Neal, you said that you "are trying to build a modern contemporary metaphorical yak poem using the kind of weaving original rhythm that Jack does in his prose." And it comes out with *Howl*.

Ginsberg: Yes about two years later. *Howl* is very definitely influenced by Jack's spontaneous method of composition. So I always found Jack extremely right, like a Zen master, and completely alone in his originality, and because of that I always hesitated to question his judgment thereafter, he always had a depth of character and appreciation that I found later on to be prophetic and useful. Same with Burroughs. I developed after a while almost too much respect perhaps, in the sense that usually I found it best to listen and absorb and learn rather than assert myself egoistically, even in respect to Jack's later political ignorance.

Le Pellec: He often referred to you as being a sort of devil.

Ginsberg: Well, I guess it's because of my devilish jealousy, or rather ignorance, in relation to his discovery of his own prose style.

Le Pellec: Wasn't it because in a way you opened to his mind fields that he didn't dare to explore?

Ginsberg: Well there was the aspect of homosexuality which, after 1947 or so, I was quite open about and familiar with and at ease in. He did not want to admit that image to his literary universe in relation to himself, and had no special reason to because he was primarily heterosexual. He had quite a bit of experience with men in bed, a lot of people blew him, even me, but he didn't particularly count it as his main métier. In fact he was sometimes a little bit patronizing of other people's homosexual sense, at other times he had a very nice mellow old-fashioned bohemian charming appreciation of it. There are many, many passages in his letters and in his writing in which he talks of going and visiting some "extraordinary charming old queen explaining the entire nature of the universe to him," you know, he had that naive appreciation of old world culture so to speak and he had even some direct contact around '46, '47, with 1933 Berlin coke-sniffing lesbian culture through some characters in Greenwich Village, and he always appreciated Burroughs of course.

Le Pellec: What do you think Burroughs brought to both of you, since he was older and was considered as a sort of teacher by the two of you?

Ginsberg: Well, first of all, the contact with an older European tradition. Burroughs had been in Europe and particularly at that crucial time described by Isherwood in *Prater Violet* and *I am a Camera:* the Berlin of Brecht and George Grosz, the glorious artistic time of the Weimar Republic in which, despite, or perhaps because of the obvious cruelty of the police state that was emerging, it was clear to more and more liberated minds how true, free, tolerant, a bohemian culture might be. Burroughs had lived in that aura and brought that over to New York. And also on the first formal visit Jack and I paid to Burroughs really to find out who he was, if he was really evil or like some sort of extraordinary melancholy blue child, he was reading a lot of books that we didn't know about and so we took our reading from him. He had Kafka's *Trial*, Cocteau's *Opium*, he had Spengler's *Decline of the West* which influenced Kerouac enormously in his prose as well as his conception of *Fellaheen*, he had Korzybski's *Science and Sanity*, so that was like a preliminary western version of the later oriental teaching of the difference between concept and suchness, between word language and actual event—he had Rimbaud's *Season in Hell*, Blake which I picked up on, he had *A Vision* by William Yeats, a sort of gnostic analysis of history and character, he had Céline's *Voyage au Bout de la Nuit* . . . If you take all those books, it takes one year or two to read them through seriously and get them all together. Burroughs had studied English and archeology at Harvard and his preoccupations were anthropological. He was interested in Kwakiutl Indian potlatch ceremonies, which I had never heard of before; in the beardoch, American Indian shamanistic transvestite figure; in the psychology of apes; in primitive mind; he was interested in the psychopath as R.D. Laing is now interested; in the crude sense that the psychopath has a certain freedom of mental conception that the so-called normal person doesn't have. So Burroughs was primarily a master of gnostic curiosities and in his approach to the mind he had the same yankee practicality and inquisitiveness as his grandfather who had invented an adding machine.

Le Pellec: He had also this orgone machine . . .

Ginsberg: He was exploring the Reichian orgone therapy. I went to a Reichian around that time myself. Burroughs was at that time being psychoanalyzed by a Doctor Federn, who had been analyzed by Freud, so he had in a sense a direct transmission to the source of psychoanalysis. And he psychoanalyzed us. I spent one year talking, free-associating on the couch everyday while Burroughs sat and listened. I really did explore a great deal of my mind and then began exploring some of my emotions. I remember bursting out in tears one day toward the end and saying "Nobody loves me!" It took a great deal of patience of Bill to sit there for a year until I bared very frail sensitive private fears. He was a very delicate and generous teacher in that way. Jack spent a good deal of time in that same relationship to Bill, being psychoanalyzed or psycho-therapized, whatever you want to call it, we didn't have to use that category, simply Bill sat and listened to us for a year. Burroughs very accurately predicted that Kerouac would move in concentric circles around his mother's apron strings until he wasn't able to go away ten feet from the house. At that time we were all living together in a house near Columbia, it was probably 1945.

Le Pellec: And Burroughs had not started writing yet?

Ginsberg: He had written one thing which was prophetic of his later work. It was a scenario called "So Proudly We Hail," which is about the sinking of the *Titanic* in which all sorts of archetypal American figures—businessmen, transvestites, schoolteachers, rich paretic millionaires—are all trapped together while the black band plays "The Star Spangled Banner." The main image of that is a syphilitic millionaire jumping in a lifeboat in women's clothes saying "Women and children first!" and cutting off with a machete the fingers of the people who wanted to climb on [laughs]. So this was his parable of the American situation. It's the basis of all his books really, he'd written it when he was at Harvard.

Le Pellec: It's typical. What about his sense of humor?

Ginsberg: Oh, exquisite. Like in *Naked Lunch.* He would tell stories and laugh [cackling to imitate Burroughs' laugh]. He and Kerouac wrote a book together by the way, around that time, called "And the Hippos Were Boiled in Their Tanks" after a news story that they heard on the radio. It was about a fire in, I think, the Saint Louis Zoo, which the announcer ended: "The fire consumed two buildings and three acres of forestland and the hippos were boiled in their tanks." Burroughs thought that this deadpan yankee bizarre image was characteristic of the most blatantly desensitized mad humor in America. Like saying "And the Vietnamese were burned alive in their huts," so to speak. So that was the title and Jack and he each wrote a chapter. It was written in the style of Raymond Chandler, hardboiled. That was very early, before *On the Road.* I think Sterling Lord has that manuscript.

Le Pellec: And Neal Cassady? He must have been very different from all of you when he arrived in New York in '46.

Ginsberg: Not much different from Jack. We were all lonely, we were solitarios, isolattoes, as Whitman said. He was different in that he just wasn't around Columbia, I suppose, but he had a lot of the knowledges that Jack was interested in: the knowledge of America particularly. He was different in the sense that we were eastern and he was from the west Rockies so he represented America to us, a child of the rainbow of the Far West, probably the same mythology that he might have represented to a Frenchman with *le mythe du Far West.* I think Neal though had a good deal more sexual experience than any of us and was much more open about it and took it as a sort of joyful yoga, and transformed it into a spiritual social thing as well as a matter of esthetic prowess. There was an element of esthetic prowess but there was also an element of faith in sexual intercourse and intimacy as an ultimate exchange of soul. That's certainly why I fell in love with him and that's why he responded to me. Because though he was primarily heterosexual, except when he was sixteen or seventeen and slept with some older people around Denver, I think he saw that I needed someone so much, because I was almost virginal and was so locked up in myself, that he sort of opened up and left himself naked and put his arms around me. He was a very beautiful open soul, very American-Whitmanic, universal in that sense. That aspect of emotional generosity and "adhesiveness" as Whitman called it was precisely the portion of Adam which had been extirpated from American public life, and even from private consciousness, in the years between Thoreau and Whitman and the post-war generations, through the development of a competitive macho capitalist selfish ethic. So Cassady was recovering a tradition of generosity of emotion and magnanimity of body and soul that were praised by Whitman and Sherwood Anderson and Hart Crane. That was really the ideal stuff of the American Adam, the image that Europe entertained, the Billy Budd that Melville had proposed, the large magnanimous citizen that Whitman proposed as necessary. It was a restoration of tenderness through the person of a definitely macho and masculine ideal western tough kid. It was a very early exhibition of that sexual democracy that's spread now and accepted by the entire psychedelic unisex generation. It's not merely a tolerance of love between men, it's a recognition of that as basic to democracy. As long as men are separate from each other and can't even touch each other, then how can they collaborate together in building a political structure? All they can do is build what we have here in America, which is this giant, robotic, criminally-dominated city culture that actually not only exploits men but in which men exploit each other, exploit women and also exploit nature. So part of our nature is affection and adhesiveness between man and man, and that had been abolished by capitalism as probably it's abolished by communism in Russia, except when everybody is drunk on vodka!

Le Pellec: You've had bad experiences in communist countries.

Ginsberg: In Cuba and Czechoslovakia, but I mean many people had bad experiences in Czechoslovakia particularly. I was banned mainly for talking like I'm talking now precisely, for talking about Whitman, talking in the Whitman party line . . . So that was Neal's particular heroism, and the interesting thing about *On the Road* and *Visions of Cody* is Kerouac's approach to Neal as a Whitmanic lover to another man and the books are real love songs of a very ancient nature. They are not to be categorized as homosexual because Jack and Neal never made love genitally, they never had sexual relations. But they had a very noble, thrilling, love tenderness, heart palpitations for each other, which is characteristic of normal masculine relationships and, as I keep saying, is almost obliterated in modern culture, probably in France as much as America now, because the machine state and the military police bureaucracy state has cultivated a paranoia between men and a suspicion and fear of body contact and soul contact in order to keep people separate, in order to divide and conquer. There is a very brilliant passage in Whitman's preface to *Democratic Vistas* that studies comradeship in political terms. [He reads a long passage from Whitman.][5] I think that is at the interesting heart of the relationship between Jack and Neal and myself and Burroughs, sometimes, as in my case and Burroughs', overtly homosexual, and in Neal's and Jack's case it's more fitting to the Adamic tradition that Whitman is proposing. But the point is that in our private relationship we found the whole spectrum of love if not convenient at least tolerable and charming. And that was a world of private sociability and discourse which was the inverse of the lack of adhesiveness and the lack of recognition of Person, the objectification, reification, depersonalization, mechanicalization of Person that made it possible for, say, the Germans to produce an Eichmann, merely following orders, or for the Americans to produce a whole generation of people who can watch U.S. wars' mass murder on television and not recognize it as personal to them. So I think *On the Road* and *Visions of Cody* and all the other books have a basic political prophetic value, not merely in discovering the body of the land, not merely in noticing the minority black superculture transcending the white superficial culture, but as the presentation for the first time in a long time of unabashed emotion between fellow citizens. And I think that sweetness of emotion is perhaps Jack's major contribution to both the literary prophetic scene in traditional American letters as well as to the generational development that's gone on since his time. And that's why his later grumpiness at left-wing anger and hostility seems somewhat relevant and in place justified, or at least understandable.

Le Pellec: Allen, there is another thing I'd like you to explain. Why did you make your breakthrough in San Francisco?

Ginsberg: Well, there was a rigidity in the N.Y. literary world here which we've described at great length already. There wasn't an admission that there was another breath in America till the early 60s. So from 1950 to 1960 the town that was most perceptive was San Francisco. It had a tradition of philosophical anarchism with the anarchist club that Rexroth belonged to, a tradition receptive to person rather than officialdom or officiousness. There already had been a sort of Berkeley Renaissance in 1948 with Jack Spicer poet, Robert Duncan poet, Robin Blaser poet, Timothy Leary psychologist, Harry Smith, great underground filmmaker, one of the people who originated the mixed media light-shows . . . They were there all around the same time, they didn't know each other well but they were passing in the street, you know. And specifically there were little magazines like *Circle* magazine, George Leite was there as an editor, there was a tradition that didn't exist in the more money-success-*Time*-magazine-oriented New York scene. There was also a gnostic tradition quite well developed in San Francisco and peyotl was understood in its place as part of the American Indian tradition. And there were a lot of interesting people: Lamantia, who had this sophisticated connection with the Surrealists—very few people in the New York professional literary world had his experience of letters, even the older people were naive compared with Lamantia—Bern Porter was there, he was an atomic physicist who quit and became a literary friend of Henry Miller, and Henry

Miller was in Big Sur, Ferlinghetti was there, with the *first* pocket paperback bookshop, so there was a whole underground tradition so to speak. That's why we had a place to publish there. For instance I took my poetry and Burroughs' *Junkie* and Jack's *On the Road* and other manuscripts around all over New York and nobody would publish them. I went to the big publishers, some of whom were friends of mine from Columbia by then, some of whom were even poets, and they rejected our books saying "The prose is bad" or, about *Junkie,* "Well that would be interesting if it were written by somebody famous like Winston Churchill" [laughs]. So I took all the manuscripts to San Francisco and began circulating them there and found a much warmer reception. Rexroth and Duncan saw them and immediately understood them as being, you know, good writing, classic. I remember Duncan's reaction to *Visions of Cody.* There's a great passage in which Kerouac goes on for pages sketching all the reflections on a curved shiny fender which was reflecting images from a plate glass window. Duncan saw that and said that anybody who could write five, or fifty pages I forget, of description of reflections in an automobile fender obviously had original genius. Whereas the reaction in New York was "What kind of mongolian idiot would even be interested in that?" or the later reaction of stupidity by Truman Capote "That's not writing, that's typewriting," superficial gaga putdown. So that's why. San Francisco was not involved with the coldest aspects of American frozen consciousness.

Le Pellec: I found that most critics tended to regard your works as manifestoes rather than as works of art. Don't you think there were some misconstructions and misunderstandings there?

Ginsberg: The works produced as literary works should be looked at as such, so that whether a consciousnes revolution is a by-product of that or is a concomitant potential of that, it doesn't come as too great a shock. They offer some sort of material base to it, being a series of verbal classics. *Howl* is not a bad poem, it's in the tradition of strong rhythmical panegyrics like Poe's "Bells" or Vachel Lindsay's "Congo" or Hart Crane's "Atlantis" or even Shelley's "Adonais." *On the Road* is a great and beautifully prosed picaresque novel of a traditional nature, *Naked Lunch* is an extension of a style already introduced and accepted as literary style by Jonathan Swift in *Gulliver's Travels* or *A Modest Proposal*. Very definitely all of our work is built on a very firm base of connaissance of twentieth-century writing from Gertrude Stein through the French Surrealists with much of their knowledge appreciated and genuflected to and then developed further in an American context for an American tongue, slightly later in the century when there was a slightly more obvious opening of a new consciousness. So it's all within the context of a known literary tradition for the French and I was surprised that it was not immediately apparent to French writers back in the 50s that what we were doing was working a further and perhaps welcome extension of their own work. Part of the dryness the French always complained about their own work of the 50s and 60s comes from that sort of lack of comradely generosity. There were nice people around; Michel Mohrt arranged for me and Burroughs to go and visit Céline in 1958. We did want to touch home-base, we did want to visit our heroes and receive their blessing and we did do that. Burroughs and Céline were like two cousins literarily and the conversation was interesting and very straight. I wrote a little bit about it in a poem called "Ignu" . . . I've always thought that we were recognizable so I wished that just the primary attention would be paid to the texts as literary texts, just so they could be inserted in the curriculum as they apparently now are, just so they would affect the consciousness of the younger generation. The longer the texts are considered as some sort of strange unicornlike objects that are not literature and not not literature, the slower the development of consciousness will be. These texts should have been around in France a long time ago.

Le Pellec: Well, they are widely read now and are published in paperback. *On the Road* for instance is being published in a new Gallimard paperback edition.

Ginsberg: That's good. See, it was the best we had in America in terms of trying to explore new territories of consciousness at a time when France, because of preoccupation with the war and perhaps exhaustion after an enormous effort earlier in the century, had come to a fixed classical overrationalistic mentality, and it was necessary for another bath of emotion and comradeship and trust.

Le Pellec: Which appeared maybe in May '68.

Ginsberg: Yes. I wish that when it appeared in May '68 it had been more informed by adhesive tenderness between men as an overt understanding, and greater experience in psychedelic modes, and some of the mellowness of character that Kerouac displays in *Doctor Sax*, the sense of Buddhist time illusion. I doubt that the revolution would have succeeded any more than it did but perhaps the effects might have been more durable if more consciousness had been reclaimed as well as more matter. But the French did astoundingly well anyway I suppose in that situation, they inspired everybody else really . . . But the conditions of revolution in late twentieth century are conditions unforeseen by any other civilization. We are going to the moon, we have drugs that go to the moon inside, we've recovered the archaic knowledges of the Australian aborigines, most primitive societies are available to us if we take the effort, many different forms of magic warfare or peacefare are available, apocalypse, classical Armageddon, destruction of the planet, millennium, all this is a possibility. So it's now unlike it ever has been in history, this should mellow everybody out and make it possible for everybody to work together, to create a revolution that had no enemies, a revolution by apokatastasis.

Le Pellec: What do you mean exactly?

Ginsberg: Apokatastasis is the transformation of satanic energy to celestial energy. In that sense the former notions are irrelevant to the revolutionary steps of consciousness that we're forced to take in order to survive without tearing the earth asunder. It means that Americans have to stop calling policemen pigs and use a different mantra on these human souls in order to transform them into helpers of the gods rather than enemies of the gods. That's the direction.

Le Pellec: Love?

Ginsberg: No, that's too much of a used word and too vague. It's more emptiness than love, detachment rather than attachment. Certainly not sentimental love. It would mean flower power, definitely, ecologically, the power of greenery to regenerate the earth. Many people have not taken into account this aspect of flower power. They think it just means sticking a blossom into the muzzle of a rifle in front of the Pentagon, but also it is the preservation of the Amazon jungle as one of the great lungs of the planet.

Le Pellec: Do you spend much time in the country now?

Ginsberg: Yea, the last four, five years. We live on a commune piece of land without electricity. We do organic farming and grow our own food. All the extra money I get I put into that, to grow food instead of spending it on plastic beer cans in the city. I don't want to be just a consumer. I consume enough paper as it is, enough electricity, so I should produce something in return, like vegetables [he goes to the kitchen and comes back holding a jar of tomatoes]. Paul Goodman showed a long time ago that the kind of industrialized farming we have is not only inhuman but is also destructive of the soil, we already saw that with the Dustbowl in the 30s. So as Goodman proposed, it would probably be useful to have decentralized specialized organic farming and that's what we are doing. It's Peter Orlovsky's work, organic farming, that's his specialty.

Le Pellec: I was surprised to see the importance young Americans grant now to the Do it Yourself thing.

Ginsberg: It's the old Thoreau tradition. The reason for that is that if you don't do it yourself you are a prisoner of the robot state, the electric company, the transportation company, the food monopolies and the chain stores. You live in a suspended state where you don't even know where your power comes from, you leave the faucets running and the lights on all night just because you don't even know that the water supplies are slowly diminishing and maybe we have only another twenty or thirty years of clean water before it all goes away. You live a situation where you let people dump your garbage out in the Atlantic Ocean so that in the last twenty years forty per cent of the life of the oceans has been destroyed.

Le Pellec: Do you think that moving out of all this is sufficient in the long run?

Ginsberg: Well, probably not but on the other hand the direction of monolithic conspicuous consumption of power and piglike abuse of natural resources both in America and Russia can only lead to planetary disaster. So now is the time for experimenting in decentralized nonpollutive power sources. And that means to some extent going back and reexamining nineteenth-century technology, miniaturizing it and making use of it in twentieth-century terms, adding a little of twentieth-century finesse and cybernetization perhaps. Nobody knows but nobody is experimenting in that area.

Le Pellec: Except in China.

Ginsberg: In China certainly. The intuitive move of many young Americans into country communes is very similar to the cultural revolution in China, when everybody was told to get out of the cities and go back to work with the workers in the fields for a while, and see what life was really like at the source of production. It's impossible for French Parisian kids or New York kids to conceive of a blueprint for a new society if they don't even know where water comes from, if they've never seen a tomato grow, if they've never milked a cow, if they don't know how to dispose of their shit, how can they possibly program a human future? It would be all abstract in their heads, like a mathematical equation, and would produce a monstrosity. Going back to the primary sources would also lead back to the people, as the Chinese said. It would also lead to a recovery of natural Adamic consciousness. It would mean the end of the noxious aspects of elitism that everybody is always complaining about, it would lead to an appreciation of the sacred character of nature that we lost, an appreciation of the American Indian virtues and earth ceremonies. Also to an appreciation of the fact that, as Gary Snyder pointed out, as in our times the exploited masses are not merely the Third World populations whose resources and labor are being stolen by the Americans who consume half of the world's raw materials with only 6 percent of the population, but the exploited masses also are the green grass, the trees, the soil, the birds, the whales and the fish, nonhuman sentient beings who are being destroyed by human greed. A funny thing to insert into Marxian ratiocination [laughs]. I think the psychedelic Marxists would understand it or it will maybe take ten years for them to realize that it's simple common sense. In 1951 Kerouac said "The earth is an Indian thing." It's very interesting that Kerouac's original preoccupation was the town and the city, the town versus the city, the monstrosity of the city and the humanity of town, and the destruction of town by mass production capitalism and hard-hearted exploitation.

Le Pellec: I found a letter from Bill Burroughs to Jack saying he knew that Jack expected to find Lowell in Mexico, which is quite in keeping with what you've just said . . .

Ginsberg: That's interesting. Cities are too horrible and are forcing people out but the main thing to do is not to see it as a mechanical exodus from an overcrowded urban madhouse but to take the opportunity then to spiritualize the country scene, get the vibrations of the trees and then come back to the city and turn the buildings into trees.

Le Pellec: Unfortunately the people who make the buildings are not those who go get the vibrations of the trees.

Ginsberg: No, people who had the power in the city always had country estates, all the way back to Louis XIV. Look at Versailles. The exploiters always dug the country.

Le Pellec: Note that in Versailles they planted orange trees to overpower the smell of their shit.

Ginsberg: That was a good idea! You don't realize the helplessness of the fat-assed, fat-bellied American Jewish boy in New York who really doesn't know how to walk and doesn't know how to climb, is short of breath and smokes too much cigarettes and eats too much meat and doesn't know how to do without electricity and doesn't know where the water comes from and thinks that his shit should go in the toilet and be flushed out into the ocean and that takes care of that. A completely hopeless creature. And it's precisely this sort of intellect, this sort of dependent, subservient, overweight mind separated from the body of the earth that was the primary critic of Kerouac when he first came on the scene with *On the Road*. They resented the holiness and wholesomeness of his body. Of course there was a lot of dewy lyricism in the book, and a lot of inexperienced joyfulness and foolish historical puns but the essential rightness and healthiness were there. And yet his work was seen by city intellectuals as being barbarian, ignorant, antisocial, anti-intellectual, mindless! Everybody was seen inside out. But the transmission of consciousness and ideas through time was already a heavy element in the original literary activity we were concerned with, in that Gary Snyder and Philip Whalen met William Carlos Williams in 1950 and learned directly from him, as I learned directly from him, as he cooperated with me, wrote prefaces to my early work and incorporated my letters to him in his *Paterson* text, as Robert Duncan and Charles Olson for many years corresponded with Pound and Williams, as Robert Creeley wrote back and forth to Pound for instructions on running a magazine when Creeley was running *Black Mountain Review* as far back as 1945, as Philip Lamantia was in connection with Breton and the Surrealists during the war in New York . . . We were carrying on a tradition, rather than being rebels. It was completely misinterpreted. We were rebelling against the academic abuse of letters but we went to the living masters ourselves for technique, information and inspiration. The academic people were ignoring Williams and ignoring Pound and Louis Zukofsky and Mina Loy and Basil Bunting and most of the major rough writers of the Whitmanic, open form tradition in America. But we had that historical continuity, from person to person. There is no gap. And since that time, this poetics has moved on into a larger democratic field even returned true lyric to pop music, through Dylan. So there's been a comradeship, a Whitmanic adhesiveness from generation to generation, from the older generation to ourselves and from ourselves to a younger group of geniuses who are reflecting our own explorations back on us and teaching us how to go further. There was a necessary democratic revolution of consciousness that I find charming and hopeful and exemplary. That sense of comradeship is what I find exemplary, and that is basically the key to what was discovered between us as a smaller group of people back in 1945.

NOTES

[1]*Blues and Haikus*, Hanover Records HM 5006 (1959). The texts are included in *Scattered Poems* (San Francisco: City Lights, 1971).

[2]Anxious about youthful emotions, guilt by association, homosexuality, political & social radicalism, anxious about the smell of self-McCarthyism, Rosenberg executions, Chambers-Hiss case, *Time* magazine's frigidities. Cigarette ads featured "men of distinction" that looked like impeccably mustached CIA agents. The code word was "Serious."

[3]By Alfred W. McCoy (New York: Harper & Row, 1973). See also *Allen Verbatim: Lectures on Poetry, Politics & Consciousness*, ed. by Gordon Ball (New York: McGraw Hill, 1975).

[4]Published in *City Lights Journal*, no. 1 (1963).

[5]See dedicatory page of *Fall of America* (San Francisco: City Lights, 1972).

A CONVERSATION

[This discussion between Paul Geneson and Allen Ginsberg took place on August 8, 1974, after a class at the Naropa Institute in Boulder. It was published in *Chicago Review*, Summer 1975.]

Paul Geneson: You say that great poetry ought to be read aloud. Or that great poetry should make it as a *spoken* thing.

Allen Ginsberg: One of the things I was trying to teach was vocalization as a practice that would lead to inspiration, defining inspiration as a function of breathing, encouraging spontaneous mind in the poetry, as Kerouac proposed it. That was like a concomitant potential of being able to breathe and to use the immediate flash material from the mind as it came up from the complete unconscious. But it definitely wasn't that great poetry *has* to be vocalized.

Geneson: I was thinking of the bardic tradition.

Ginsberg: Yes, what I was really interested in was this aspect of improvisation rather than vocalization. But of course improvisation requires vocalization. There are some poets who make use of the page like a painting, like Apollinaire, and that's interesting. But the main line of poetry is the breath, not the page.

Geneson: In *Howl* you wrote about one writing off the top of one's head, going on and on, which in the morning was "gibberish."

Ginsberg: I was thinking of amphetamine head-babbling—"which in the yellow morning were stanzas of gibberish." I was thinking about poems that I'd written on benzedrine back in 1948. The specific problem I had was, my mind would get tangled at the end and I'd begin revising, and by the time I was done, the last few climactic pages of any long poem written on amphetamine would

be this chicken track, this patchwork that I couldn't decipher any more. So, in other words, I was talking very specifically about *that*, but I didn't mean "spontaneity doesn't make it."

Geneson: Well, regarding revision itself you mentioned that you do revise, but not extensively. You mentioned the haiku . . .

Ginsberg: Well, all my poetry is completely revised.

Geneson: . . . the idea of haiku, where it just comes out. The idea of haiku being revised . . .

Ginsberg: Not supposed to be, really. I think the haiku-composing situation is a group of people with sake, or tea, or if there's old friends visiting from another province, and they've just met, or they're going away, and they're sitting around at a poignant moment, and there's a full moon, and it's winter, summer, spring, or autumn. They have brushes and ink, and it's esthetically pleasing, and they mix the ink and amuse each other, charm each other, or get drunk meanwhile running down thoughts they have about the poignancy of the moment, whether the butterfly flew into the room and stumbled into the green tea and drowned, or whether the moon had just risen, or whether the fly came on the rice and they didn't have to chase him off because they had plenty of rice. So the very situation makes it spontaneous, it's a poetry-writing party, where you have, you know, a thought and you write it down. It's like you play the guitar. Or like, say, some of the Black bluesmen here in America sitting around in somebody's kitchen in Memphis and maybe somebody has played a blues, somebody else picks up on the tune and adds stanzas, and they didn't even write it down, much less revise it.

But I talking about the introduction of courage and openness in the writing so that you'd realize you were already in eternity while you were living on earth, for the first and last time, and whatever you said at that moment was whatever you said at that moment. So in a sense you couldn't change, you could go on to another moment. It's best not, in a way, to circle back. I remember Robert Duncan got up and walked [Ginsberg gets up and walks several feet in one direction, then returns] across the room and then said, "After I've walked, how can I change my step?" How can you revise what you've written? Writing is like walking, like any act.

Geneson: Yet you do revise your poems?

Ginsberg: I don't write until I revise first, whatever that means. I'm *sick* of saying I don't revise, so maybe I'll say I revise all the time. At this point what I've been doing in the last two years' readings, every reading, or every other reading, I improvise a poem on the stage, and that's usually the best part of the reading, for me.

Geneson: In conversation this summer Nelson Algren said that Kerouac had written some good things, but that his spontaneity, and the long line, was too much. You've felt Kerouac to be an influence.

Ginsberg: Yeah, I guess the biggest influence on me. My favorite work is *Mexico City Blues*, which is poetry, and *Visions of Cody*, which was never even published then (it's now published and sold out its first edition, another "underground" classic, posthumously). His solidest work, in a way, is *Big Sur*.

Geneson: What I'm leading to is the question of why this long line has been so difficult to assimilate.

Ginsberg: That's not true. Look at Thomas Wolfe. Kerouac got it from Thomas Wolfe, and from Herman Melville, and from Walt Whitman, and from the Bible, and from Shakespeare, and from Rabelais, Sir Thomas Browne, Burton.

Geneson: In American poetry could you say the long line has been a sort of major poetic?

Ginsberg: Yes, you can. From Whitman, Robinson Jeffers, and myself. From Edward Carpenter, whom you don't know. From Marsden Hartley. Just a long, long, long, long, long line. It's one of the major forms among the younger poets in New York and San Francisco. Like in Ashbery or Koch.

Geneson: Yes, but that's a shorter long line than, say, your long line or Kerouac's long line.

Ginsberg: But actually we're confusing a couple of things. A long line is open form, right? Open form, or spontaneous style. There's a couple of elements we're considering. I write short lines too. Most of my stuff, besides *Howl* and *Kaddish*, is Williamsesque, short line. But we were talking about Kerouac and Kerouac's

long line. If you look at American literature, you'd have to say, Melville and Whitman, *there's* American literature, Melville and Whitman. And there's short, spontaneous lines like Emily Dickinson and Kerouac. It's a basic practice, because it relates to the breath. And because it relates to great inclusiveness of mind that can enjamb—put in one breath a great many associations. Which is what Eliot finally decided about Milton's line, that Milton could go from Heaven to Hell in one—

> Him the almighty power
> Hurled headlong flaming from the ethereal sky
> With hideous ruin and combustion down
> To bottomless perdition, there to dwell
> In adamantine chains and penal fire,
> Who durst defy the omnipotent to arms.

—from Heaven to Hell in one line, and all the way through in between. So in his later essay on Milton, and on the great blind musicians Milton and Joyce, Eliot noticed that they had this enormous syntactical line that could cover whole worlds of association in one sentence, in one *think*, in one breath. That was Kerouac's purpose, and that's what's great about Melville. So a long line is one of the major forms from the Bible on up to Hart Crane—

> O thou steeled Cognizance whose leap commits
> The agile precincts of the lark's return;
> Within whose lariat sweep encinctured sing
> In single chrysalis the many twain,—
> Of stars Thou art the stitch and stallion glow
> And like an organ, Thou, with sound of doom—
> . . . .
> Sustained in tears the cities are endowed
> And justified conclamant with ripe fields
> revolving through their harvests in sweet torment.

See, Kerouac got his line from people like Crane, Melville, and Walt Whitman: *that* big breath. That was what I liked about Kerouac, that was what turned me on to *Howl* from Kerouac's writing, from *Visions of Cody*, actually. It was this tremendous beauty of outpouring, really, the full heart.

Geneson: That's kind of what I was thinking about, that in your

long line, in Kerouac's long line, there's this tremendous exu ance, this praise. A lot of it is not only reaching out in prais humanity, also a reaching out and saying, look at this countr

Ginsberg: This is associated with the Open Road.

Geneson: Yeah, and I wonder why it is that today people ar writing a kind of exuberant poetry about traveling, about country.

Ginsberg: There are lots of young people who do have t breath.

Geneson: But the attitude of discovering America . . . .

Ginsberg: The localism and appreciation of native roots, mair through Williams and Kerouac, has woken everybody up to t beauty of Lawrence, Kansas, or Omaha, Nebraska. And ever body's got a humorous, tragic view of their own hometown b cause of taking *acid* there. So the big city is no longer mecca, an there's a longhaired move to the country, the more remote fr the police-state the better. You're out in the woods. And there also this, in a sense, the fall of America as a nation-state and th fall of any national concept. And an appreciation of the Amer Indian vision of America as "Turtle Island," the actual land, like in Hart Crane, rather than in America like in Whitman, o Kerouac, or myself. They've transcended America now; everybody digs their locality at this point.

Geneson: Digs where they are?

Ginsberg: Where they *came* from. I mean partly out of the simple political and social awareness that centralization is a failure, is a loss, a loser. And that decentralized energy forms, and decentralized cultural forms are, are, as Williams always points out, the richest. They had a local tradition and are rooted in the actua land. So that there's less a movement, say, to violently "challenge" people's Provincial Notions, in the South, and more of a movement to enlighten, or illuminate them, or mediate them out or zap them out in mind essence. Those kids going back are thinking more in terms of country wisdom and *learning* from the people they "hate."

Geneson: Now there seems to be, on the college campus, a going

backward. They like Ike, they like Nixon.

Ginsberg: Oh, come on. You're speaking on the very day Nixon is resigning, and the majority of the American public is saying he ought to resign or be impeached. Remember it got to be like a crisis about a year ago of mass hallucination after the election where Nixon had successfully propagandized and brainwashed and got himself elected, and then there was, slowly, for some reason or other, a whole psychological turning around of the country. A major center of bullshit has been wiped out; what's been abandoned, I think, is the rhetorical violence and impractical aspect of revolutionary stones thrown at cops, but that's all to the good. People are digging in for a longer haul.

I think that the *idea* of a return to conservatism was part of a well-orchestrated image plot by the advertising industry and Nixon to brainwash people, and I think your acceptance of that idea is part of a brainwash rather than a perception of what is actually going on. Because what's actually going on, I think, is a really much deeper research into one's own spiritual and emotional nature, and an examination, on the part of the "movement," of its own aggression in order to gain much deeper revolutionary power, or change power. I think the die has been cast, and America can't ever be the same again. And Nixon's resignation isn't very important, because everybody's now so disillusioned. So it isn't as if everybody's *illusioned* again with Eisenhower-Nixon. Everybody's *so* disillusioned that it doesn't really make any difference.

We'll just slowly adjust. We'll probably start gardening more, and probably the cities will stop their growth, and there'll be a decline in population a little bit, and more people will go to the country, and there'll be some pressure for land reform. I mean, it's simply, the economics would require that.

Geneson: You mentioned in an earlier interview "magic phrases."

Ginsberg: Oh, I was probably talking about "Wichita Vortex Sutra," and the use of the statements of poetry as mantra for "magical" effects.

Geneson: And you said, I think . . .

Ginsberg: "I here declare the end of the war," was that it?

Geneson: Yeah, I think you said that once these things are said it's as if something is touched in everyone's unconscious. Like "Impeach Nixon" was there, but needed to be said.

Ginsberg: "What oft was thought, but ne'er so well expressed."

Geneson: And today, are there a multitude of magic phrases, will they come out, are they coming out now?

Ginsberg: Did I use that phrase?

Geneson: Yes, I think, "magic phrase," "magical phrase"—I'm not sure. What kind of magical phrase could you use today that's comparable to "I here declare the end of the war"?

Ginsberg: "Work, work, work, this inspiration proves that I have dreamed."

Genesen: But what kind of statement today could have a reverberation similar to the one about ending the war?

Ginsberg: Oh, well okay, I thought of it last night. "Even the President of the United States must someday stand naked."

Geneson: Which is Dylan.

Ginsberg: Yes. Dylan's statement was one of the many, many things that brought that about. I'm sure that Dylan can be given credit for this particular view of Nixon that everybody is having right now. I'm sure Dylan is as responsible as . . . Senator Ervin. I mean just the suggestion that Dylan made and inserted into public consciousness altered people's thinking and prepared the way for the kind of mentality that could go through Watergate. So I would say "Even the President of the United States must stand naked" was like a mantric phrase which woke a certain insight up in people, because they knew it but they didn't. And I think people started thinking in those terms, Nixon couldn't get away with his mystification; that line demystified the authority of the Oval Office.

Geneson: Why is it today that poetry has become so involved with *personal* experience? Where are the political satires?

Ginsberg: Well, Michael McClure's political and social and biological satires, which are playing in San Francisco now and which are probably great classics. I'll tell you what I'm interested in. I'm interested in meditation, in exploring inner space, in a certain political movement which would involve a sit-in in Washington, where hundreds of thousands of people would just go to Washington and sit down. Ten hours on Monday, for ten days, ten hours a day, doing nothing but sitting. I'd like to see that. That many people doing nothing would create such a pool of nothing-doing that it just wouldn't contribute to the aggression that's going around. I'd like to see Nixon sit down and do nothing for a while and take a rest, stop working so hard.

Geneson: I haven't heard you talk much about Wallace Stevens.

Ginsberg: Yeah, I like his later poems, "The Rock" particularly. There's a great line [in "Lebensweisheitspielerei"]—

> Weaker and weaker, the sunlight falls
> . . . .
> Those that are left are the unaccomplished,
> The finally human,
> Natives of a dwindled sphere.

—and then the verse ends

> In the stale grandeur of annihilation.

That's a great line: "In the stale grandeur of annihilation"—like Shakespeare's lines.

Geneson: Stevens had an idea in which each person is constantly formulating and reformulating his own poem about reality.

Ginsberg: That probably happens.

Geneson: Pound seemed to need the stimulus of living abroad. Would you say that you write better here in America? You wouldn't say that any one place is any better than another?

Ginsberg: Well, I'm partial to local particularity, after my guru William Carlos Williams, to working grassroots and using local speech and local dialect and local fact, and having poetry related to the actual backbreaking work where you are.

Geneson: Are you now living in the West?

Ginsberg: I've been all summer in the West, living on the same land with Gary Snyder. We're building a little "cottage in the western night." [The discussion comes to focus on Ginsberg's plans for organizing a school of poetics within the Naropa Institute at Boulder, Colorado.] I don't know what we'll call it. School of Spontaneous Mind Poetics, or something. Kerouac Memorial Academy. Burroughs Academy. What we're thinking of setting up is something run by poets, actually, an arts school. It would involve poetics based on classical principles of open form, that is, the Japanese tradition of the haiku, which we were describing, and improvisation of Milarepa, the great Tibetan saint poet, like Indian *mushaira* forms where poets simply get together with wine and moonlight and their instruments and cap each other with songs. Or the American tradition of the improvised blues. We'll see if we can find some great traditional blues singers, like Furry Lewis. Dirty, improvised blues—which is some of the most deeply-rooted and least acknowledged—if you look at anthologies of blues texts, you'll find people like Furry Lewis.

Geneson: That does seem to be a sort of sub-stream of American poetry.

Ginsberg: I think it's a major stream, not in the academy, but if you look back a hundred years you'll find that it was the most influential form of poetics, that it influenced the entire world, and that when the anthologies get rewritten, any major anthology of American poetry would have to include—

I'll give you sugar for sugar
                    And you'll get salt for salt
I'll give you sugar for sugar
                    But you'll get salt for salt
Baby if you don't love me
                    It's your own damn fault

Sometimes I think that you're too sweet to die
Sometimes I think that you're too sweet to die
And other times I think you ought to be buried alive.

Richard "Rabbit" Brown. So I think that Amiri Baraka's (LeRoi Jones') complaint that the strongest forms of the American art which have Black roots have been *shut out* from serious study by the academies is completely true. So we have to found an academy that would include the "mainstream" of American poetry. I think that's a good deal more important than an overemphasis on Wallace Stevens.

Geneson: But Black poetry—

Ginsberg: I'm not talking about "Black poetry." I'm talking about Calypso and blues . . .

Geneson: Yeah, workers . . .

Ginsberg: Not workers—they were great musicians. "Black girl, black girl, don't lie to me/ Tell me where did you sleep last night" is as good as any ancient English lyric. As good as "Lord Randall." "In the pines, in the pines/ Where the sun never shines/ I shivered the whole night through." That's a perfect "lyric" because it's to be sung.

Geneson: But isn't that derived, you know, people from people, from workers, not academicians?

Ginsberg: Well, it was not an academic form. But then, *at that time* (1925), if you look at the anthologies made by academicians, you find that the great nominees for anthological immortality were Trumbull Stickney, Archibald, uh—Cox—[laughs] I don't know, Archibald *Rut*ledge. Have you ever heard of Archibald Rutledge?

Geneson: No, I haven't.

Ginsberg: Well, there was an anthology that my father used in college put together by the Superintendent of Education of all New England,[1] or something, that gave thirty pages to Archibald Rutledge and three pages to Walt Whitman—Whitman's "Pioneers, O Pioneers." And of course at that time, when blues was at its height, there was absolutely no attention to it as poetics. I mean you can go back to the eighteenth century, you know, Pope and Johnson complaining of poetasters. And you go back to the old arguments about the poet laureate. The official poetry, the poetry that was considered poetry in Blake's time, didn't have anything to do with what was really going on, as we know now by hindsight. And when you add in the tremendous mass of texts of blues songs and all these forms you get an astounding enlargement of the canon. There's a really great book that came out a couple of years ago, called *The Blues Line,*[2] which took all the great blues lyrics, not the music, and arranged them on the page according to breath stop, according to principles of Olson's projective verse, so that the whole page looks like a page of Pound, or Williams, indicating the breath stops. It's a very *modern* poetry. Of course it is all vocal, and therefore capable of division on a page as modern poetry is divided, line by line, measured by breath on the page. And it's like Tottel's *Miscellany* or Percy's *Reliques*.

Geneson: But hasn't a lot of this poetry been class-dominated, certain classes could not get recognition for their poetry?

Ginsberg: It's partly class-dominated and partly what Pound complained about, a domination by academic bureaucrats who are not themselves poets, but who are making a living out of the *energy* of poetry.

Geneson: You mentioned, in another interview, E. A. Robinson as a person who was in your father's anthology.

Ginsberg: Yeah, he was the greatest of them, you know, among that rhymed lyric mode because he wrote some very great "poems." "Eros Tyrannos," you know that? Those were standard in high school when I was going to high school. But it's finally a dead form, I think, in the sense that he was writing in forms that were meant to be sung, like Dylan, but he just wasn't a singer. He was a guy with, like, a stiff collar and big, round eye-glasses.

Geneson: Finally, will you teach, or could you consider yourself teaching, in an academic situation, in the academy?

Ginsberg: Academy means, literally, a grove of trees, where people walked and talked with their teacher, as Philip Whalen pointed out. In American University-academies you now have plastic halls. In the Platonic Academy students and teachers lived together, teaching was founded on relationship between poetry and mind—and poetry was *practiced*. That's my ideal, anyway. If it were customary for the Chair of Poetics to be occupied by B.B. King or Furry Lewis or Leadbelly, then OK for Academy. But it isn't customary, most Academies see poetry teaching in terms of analytic criticism, rather than live creation. I like the archiving nature of the Academy, but more inspiration is necessary in the XX Century grove—then poetry be teachable.

NOTES

[1] *American Poetry*, edited by A. B. De Mille (Boston: Allyn and Bacon, 1923, o.p.).

[2] *The Blues Line*, compiled by Eric Sackheim (New York: Schirmer Books paperback, 1975).

"FIRST THOUGHT, BEST THOUGHT"

[From Allen Ginsberg's Spiritual Poetics class July 29, 1974. First published in *Loka, 1: A Journal from Naropa Institute* (1975).]

Allen Ginsberg: I was thinking of something Robert Duncan told me in 1963 when I was singing Hare Krishna. He found that I was using my voice and my body a lot more thickly and a lot more involved than I was when reading poetry. That I was putting more force and more energy and more conviction into the physical rendering of the mantras than I was into what I was supposed to be good at, which was the poetry. Which I think was a real criticism, a seed that stuck a long time and flowered, because from then on I realized that singing is a really good thing, if it can bring that out, and break the shyness or the barrier of fear of energy, or fear of expression. But also it made me conscious of the fact that whatever really great poetry I wrote, like *Howl* or *Kaddish*, I was actually able to chant, and use my whole body, whereas in lesser poetry, I wasn't, I was talking. Or, I shouldn't say lesser, but poetry that didn't involve me as much: so in that sense, lesser. So from that point of view, poetry becomes less intellectual or verbal and also becomes a physiological thing. Something where you actually use your body, use your breath, use your full breath. At least chant becomes that—and poetry can approach chant, or poetry when you're really into it can become an expression of the whole body, "single body, single mind," with real *oomph*, as distinct from the practice of poetry as it was all along in my day and probably yours still, which is more of a tentative thing where you're dealing with flimsy materials of your own mind and so you're not really sure whether you should lay it out solid like a prophet, or whether it's worth shouting or speaking or howling, or using your whole self in. That's not, of course, the only form of poetry, because there's a quiet conversational poetry, and there's a whispered poetry, and I guess whispered transmissions even, but that area of full energy is very rarely appreciated now. It's appreciated when you hear it; when you hear it in Dylan, it's totally appreciated, which is the great thing about Dylan—he puts his whole lung in one vowel: "How does it *FEEL*," or as in old blues, "HOME, I'm going HOME,"[1] so you have the whole body into it because what is meant is something very definite emotionally, rather than tentative.

So, it's good then to link poetics with some form of vocalization. Also, I began the class today, somewhat thoughtlessly, shrewdly, with vocalizing the mantra AH, so we're all vocalizing together with some spirit. And in a way, it would be ideal if the poetry we arrive at by writing could involve us joyfully, "livelyly," —could involve us enough so that we could recite our own poetry with the same kind of spirit as we sing. We sing kind of abandoned —we could dig our poetry as much, actually dig our own utterances, as much as we do our own nonsensicals, our chanting. It's a state that I've sort of arrived at over the years with my own poetry, and I've seen other poets arrive at also. I think it's a good deal, a good thing to keep in mind, because otherwise you get immediately the danger of bawling out bullshit or reciting in a high cracked, tense, nervous voice or a tearful voice, an overtearful voice, or oversentimental, tearful voice. Reciting, "Bullshit, the police are after me, my best friend was busted, where are all the roses?" Which was typical of the poetry of the early 60s. Overgeneralized, but shouted.

So that's the obvious danger, but if you noticed, the voice came somewhere from the top of the throat rather than the center of the body. That's another interesting technical matter for voice, for the vocalization of poetry—that the best poets I've heard, orators, say, do speak from their whole body. Someone who commands attention and authority—it's a very subtle thing, it's not so much what they're saying, it's that the voice does come from the center of the body, from say the heart chakra, which is a learnable thing. I mean, it's something that's developable, when you become conscious of it, when you do a lot of chanting. I think it develops naturally when you solidify and mature.

So there's vocalization, but to have vocalization, you've got to have vowels, vowels make the vocalization easy. You've got something to vocalize, with a vowel you can use your whole lung.

What is that called technically? The assonance. The repeated musical use of vowels. Which they also used to teach, but they didn't teach how much fun it is, or they didn't teach that it was a form of yoga, or maybe they did, but I wasn't listening. People who are mentally hung up on what they are saying, and too careful in what they are saying, and not relying enough on their body and spontaneous mind, generally fail to appreciate the solidity and strength of their own organlike tones, and fail to appreciate that they can really swing with vowels also. Because if you want to give yourself something to work with, poetically, while writing, just remember "a, e, i, o, u,—a, e, i, o, u," or any variation of the vowels.

And for that, if you look at any of the great classic poetic warhorses, like "The Bells" or Shelley's "Adonais" or "Epipsychidion" or *Paradise Lost*—a lot of really interesting vibrant, vibratory, stanzaic poetry or blank verse—you find that it's really solid chunks of vowels that you can get your glottis into, or whatever vowels issue from. One that my father taught me when I was young—some lines from *Paradise Lost*—I remember often:

> Him the almighty power
> Hurled headlong flaming from the ethereal sky
> With hideous ruin and combustion down
> To bottomless perdition, there to dwell
> In adamantine chains and penal fire,
> Who durst defy the omnipotent to arms.

It was just a great voice exercise. I didn't see it as such, I just saw it as a great streak of bopping, I guess. I never saw my father come on like that otherwise you know, with such great vocal fire, vocal force, with such breath—I mean it was nice to see my father so *animated*. Is there a relationship between the root word of "animated" and "breath"? I guess "soul" and the breath links up there somewhere. Soul is breath, in a way, they say.

The title of this course is Spiritual Poetics, which was just a spontaneous title arrived at when we had to have a title, but might as well be used. We're beginning with considerations of breath, considerations of vowel, and relation between vowel and intelligence, vowel and soul,—and how these are connected to the breath. As here, say with Chögyam's[2] teaching, "Ah" is a basic mantra—"Ah" as the exhalation of the breath, as appreciation of the breath also. Appreciation of the empty space into which breath flows. The *open* space, into which breath flows.

So if we're talking poetics, and beginning with breath, the vowel road is connected then with the title of the course, Spiritual Poetics. And the mantric aspect is a lot more important than has been understood in western poetry—as pure breath, as exhalation of breath, as articulation of breath, as manifestation of breath, as animation, as expression in really the easiest and most natural way of your own nature, which is by breathing, and making a sound while breathing. Just like the wind makes a sound in the leaves. No more presumptuous than the wind in the leaves. Of course, no more honorable either. But at any rate, not guilty. No more guilty than the wind in the leaves. So if you take that approach, that your singing or your chanting or your poetics is as neutral, impersonal, and objective as the wind through the black oak leaves, then you wouldn't have to be ashamed of expressing yourself, because it's not yourself, it's just the wind, it's just wind, it's just breath going through you. Then you might take the trouble to fit it to whatever your subjective intellect is thinking about at the moment, and you might take the trouble to link that breath up with whatever is going on in your mind at the moment, or to what you remember is going on in your mind or your body at the moment. But that can be done as spontaneously as breathing, in the sense that the mind is always working—it's hard to stop, as those of you who have been meditating know.

How many here sit? So, nearly everybody. So we all know the experience of observing our minds moving and listening to chatter and gossip, discursive thought, not being able to stop, and maybe not even needing to attempt to stop it, simply observing it. I've lately come to think of poetry as the possibility of simply articulating that, in other words, observing your mind, remembering maybe one or two thoughts back and laying it out. So in that sense it's as easy as breathing because all you're doing is listening to particulars, those particulars of what you were just thinking about. And in that respect, it's very close to meditation. Meditation is good practice for poetry. In other words, it's not the opposite, it's not an enemy of poetry. It was formerly seen to be, occasionally, by various hung-up intellectuals, who were afraid that they'd be silent, and they wouldn't be able to be poets then. But actually all it does is give you lots of space and place in time to recollect what's going on in your mind, so providing lots of material, lots of ammunition, lots of material to work with.

So if you are practicing in the line of Gertrude Stein and Kerouac, spontaneous transcription, transmission of your thought, how do you choose then what thoughts to put down? The answer is that you don't get a chance to choose because everything's going so fast. So it's like driving on a road; you just have to follow the road. And take turns, "eyeball it," as a carpenter would say. You don't have any scientific measuring rod, except your own mind, really. I don't know of any scientific measuring rod that's usable. So you just have to chance whatever you can and pick whatever you can. So there's also a process of automatic selection. Whatever you can draw in your net is it, is what you got—whatever you can remember, and whatever you can manage physically to write down is your poem, or is your material. And you've got to trust that, sort of as the principle of selection, so you have to be a little athletic about that, in the sense of developing *means* of transcription, ease of transcription, overcoming resistance to transcription.

Student: Does that also have to do with what you choose to use, either typing, or writing, or tape recorder?

Ginsberg: Yeah, very much so. I want to go into that anyway, in just a minute. First I want to get to the nub of selection, because that used to be a big academic argument about "the principle of selectivity" and of "'Beaknik' writers being unselective," and that "selection was absolutely important," that you really had to make fine distinctions between different kinds of thoughts and only choose the loftiest thoughts, or the most poetic thoughts, and you had to intercede or intervene in your mind with another mind from somewhere else, someone else's mind really, Lionel Trilling's mind or Allen Tate's mind, or Brooks and Warren's mind, the critics' minds. You had to use somebody else's mind or some objective mind to choose among the thoughts, but I think that's too hard, I think that's too much work. It'll only get you tangled up in a feedback loop of some sort, because you forget what you were thinking, and you'll think what you were supposed to be thinking. So the problem is to stay with what you were really thinking instead of what you think you're supposed to be thinking.

So from that point of view, I would say that the only thing you can get down is what you can remember and what you can write down: in other words, the actual process of writing, the physical process of writing or vocalizing or tape-recording or babbling spontaneously—that physical activity determines what gets laid out on the paper or on the air. It's a pretty good critic, because the mind somehow or other, if you leave it alone a little bit and accept it, tends to select its own society, tends to cling to obsessions and preoccupations. Recurrent thoughts finally do get out, things that are really recurrent do come up and are rememberable. And one really difficult part is that there's a tendency toward censorship—that some thoughts seem too embarrassing, too raw, too naked, too irrelevant, too goofy, too personal, too revealing, too damaging to one's own self-image, too cranky, too individualistic, too specialized, or too much fucking your mother or something, so that you don't want to put them down. That's a real problem with everybody, including myself. The *pudeur*, modesty, shyness—like I failed to write down a dream the other day. Fortunately, I remembered it—I saw Peter Orlovsky catch me smoking, and he's very much antismoking. We were living together, and in the dream he was so dismayed that he vomited up his liver, and I realized that I was really violating something sacrosanct and rooted, physiologically rooted in him, in something real. And I got so scared of the domestic situation that I didn't write the dream down. But it was actually one of the more interesting dream-poem possibilities that I'd had in the last month.

But in the moment of writing, there'll be all sorts of images rise, "thinks," separate "thinks" that will be unappetizing, and I think that's the most important part. The parts that embarrass you the most are usually the most interesting poetically, are usually the most naked of all, the rawest, the goofiest, and strangest and most eccentric and at the same time, most representative, most universal, because most individual, most particular, most specific, vomiting out a piece of liver, specific situation, smoking. Actually, I thought that was really just my scene, but really it's universal, it's an archetype, as much as anything's an archetype. And that was something I learned from Kerouac, which was that spontaneous writing could be embarrassing, or could seem to be embarrassing. So the cure for that is to write things down which you will not publish and which you won't show people. To write secretly, to write for nobody's eye, nobody's ear but your own, so you can actually be free to say anything that you want. In other words, it means abandoning being a poet, abandoning any careerism, abandoning even the idea of writing any poetry, really abandoning, giving up as hopeless—abandoning the possibility of really expressing yourself to the nations of the world. Abandoning the idea of being a prophet with honour and dignity, and abandoning the glory of poetry and just settling down in the muck of your own mind. And the way that's practiced is that you take it out a week later and look at it. It's no longer embarrassing, it seems by that time funny. The blood has dried, sort of. So you really have to make a resolution just to write for yourself, but really for yourself, in the sense of no bullshit to impress others, in the sense of not writing poetry to impress yourself, but just writing what your self is saying.

My own experience with *Howl* was precisely that. After writing some very formalistic poetry, I decided I'd let loose whatever I wanted to let loose with and say what I really had on my mind and not write a poem, finally—break my own forms, break with my own ideals, ideas, what I was supposed to be like as a poet and just write whatever I had in mind. And once written, I realized it could never be published, because it would offend too many people, I thought, particularly my family. Which I think is a problem Kerouac had too. He was afraid his mother would read his secret thoughts and disapprove of his friends, or sexual activities, or dope-smoking or beatnik habits, or something—the drinking, who knows, the snot, his masturbation, whatever.

It's a common occurrence, especially among younger poets, to find that the form of writing that they didn't conceive of as their main thing, their main *schtick*, their main poem—like notes to themselves, or their journal, or letters or just sort of banjo-chanting by themselves, or chanting to themselves while walking across Brooklyn Bridge, or on mountaintops—was actually more interesting, later on, than the stuff they prepared as poetry. And I found that in my case to be so. For years I wrote very formal rhymed verse, and at the same time was keeping a very loose, erratic journal, very similar to a journal that I published called *Indian Journals*. A journal which I've kept continually from 1946 on. And I found that little fragments from the journal were more hot than anything I'd written down or prepared and rhymed and poetised with the idea of writing poetry. So it's almost like if you can catch yourself not writing poetry, but writing down what you're really thinking, actually, you arrive at a genuine piece of writing, of self-expression. And that may be more interesting than what you're careeristically considering as your poems. So one of the technical aids would be to stick to poems that you're not going to publish, so that you're really free to write down what you want to write.

Student: Do you find that even transcribing straight thoughts tends to focus your attachment to your thoughts?

Ginsberg: What do you mean by "focus your attachment"?

Student: I found that in keeping a journal I got so attached to thoughts, so aware of thoughts, that I actually was subtly manufacturing more of them to make a more pleasing journal.

Ginsberg: Yeah, well, there's a certain amount of baroque elegance that can be indulged in—playfulness—if it's playful enough it's all right. Sometimes. That's just sheer abundance, and playfulness, but while you're doing that, sometimes there's something else going on, an undertow of real thought that you've got to pay attention to. So maybe you start getting baroque, and then interrupt it—just break it off in the middle, be playful and break it off in the middle. William Carlos Williams used a dot for an unfinished sentence, for an unfinished thought—a dot spaced out, like a period, but in the middle of a line. Or a dash could be used, as Hart Crane did in a really interesting poem which you might look up, "Havana Rose," which was like a drunken suicide note to himself. It was one of the things that turned me on to *raw thought* as poetry. A little free-associational piece, like the kind of note you might write to yourself drunk, which wasn't meant as a poem, which was recovered from his papers, and it's one of his most charming, personal pieces.

Student: How do you use those fragments of thoughts as material —what are you using them as material for?

Ginsberg: They're the poem. You don't have to "work" any more on it. That's it. You don't have to do any more work. No, the whole process of poetry is totally without any work at all. It should be, I think. At least to *begin* with. There might be some work later on, but until you establish this basis of honesty, I don't think it's worth working on anything beyond that. It takes a lot of practice just to get down what you've got. You can worry about it later. I mean it's really so charming and hard. I mean I can't do it that often, actually *catch* myself and write it down. You can't do it once a day or once every week, or once a month even, *really* catch yourself thinking something interesting. Then if you can do one little four-line fragment a month, you've got it made for the rest of your life, you realize, you'd do better than Sappho. As *much* as Sappho, as much as Anacreon. Actually if you're young when you start out, just four lines a month and you've built up a total body of work, by the end of your lifetime you're too much to read. And you can do five minutes a day, practicing five minutes a day, writing, oddly enough, more than anybody wants to read.

Student: Does that mean catching yourself as interesting?

Ginsberg: Well, interesting because clear, because definite, because *there,* because you really did catch yourself. Unwittingly catch yourself. In a moment you didn't quite like, or maybe did like a lot. So that brings up, how do you catch yourself? And how to be prepared to catch yourself. Which brings up the question about materials. What you use for transcription. What I use basically is this pocket notebook. Generally, I use maybe one a month, or one every two months. Twenty-nine cents and a nineteen cent ball point pen, the only investment you need. That's for moving around, for traveling, for getting thoughts on the wing. "Dinosaur, cancer, Buchenwald, hellrat, heavy metal, sweet oleanders down the middle of the strip of the freeway." Well, that was part of a conversation with Gary Snyder. And the title is, "On the way to pick up Peter in the Sacramento airport," or "I'm going to pick up Peter Sacto Airport." June 1—not much of an entry.

Student: During meditating, do you ever stop and jot down some of the neat things that happen?

Ginsberg: Well, sometimes I take my notebook to meditation and I sneak in a couple of lines or go to the bathroom.[3] I was in Wyoming at the seminary sitting for three months, from September to December last year, and I had the little notebook and a couple of times I interrupted the sitting to write something down. Neruda had died—I had read it in the paper before I went in to sit, and I was thinking about breathing, and— "Some breath breathes out Atlantis, Adonais, some breath breathes out bombs, and dog barks, some breath breathes over Rendezvous Mountain, some breath breathes not at all." I thought, "Gee, that's funny, Neruda's not breathing, so breath breathes not at all." It was so mysterious and strange, that thought, that I pulled out my notebook and wrote it. It's enough. It sat there—and that was the end of my thought. So if I wanted another poem, another thought would be another poem. And that was a very definite end. I mean, what else, you can't go on from there. So breath breathes not at all.

Student: Do you think it's possible to go back to something you wrote earlier?

Ginsberg: I don't know if you could intentionally do it but you might find yourself back, particularly if the place where you were was a basic place. And so you'd naturally go back there. I mean, basic in terms of your feelings, your sitting, breathing, your posture, your appreciation of your eyeballs, your appreciation of space in front of you, the wonder of being there again, in the body, sitting, breathing—that's a place you always go back to when you're sitting, or sometimes when you're writing. But then the content—*that* you could never go back to, the freshness of that knowledge.

Student: Do you ever find a few fragments that were separate for a long time, and then you realized that they were connected?

Ginsberg: If they were related, I'd put them one, two, three, four. And have done so. In college I used to try to tie them together in big formal poems, but it was fakery. And I got more and more interested in just the bare bones of the process as being enough. As being more exemplary, teaching more to other people, and at the same time, teaching me more, and at the same time being more honest. And less weighty, less heavy. Less heavy-handed, less ambitious, less egotistical. And also, you know, there's an awful lot of writing anyway. More writing than anybody can read. You know, the swifter we are at it, the better. You get more chance of being read if you just stick to what you know, rather than trying to construct something you don't know. Though, in the process of constructing something using your spontaneous mind playing, there's also that element of invention and comedy and friendliness that issues forth.

What I'm trying to do is sort of describe the narrow path of practice to get to the mind. How far in the mind we get depends really on the application of practice, the application of meditation, the sincerity of practice, the clarity of the practice as distinct from the ambitiousness of it. The simplicity of the practice as distinct from the greediness of it.

Student: But won't that process continue forever, if you are just writing what your mind is thinking, without any focus of a religious nature? Won't you always be writing about the garbage in your mind?

Ginsberg: Well, you're assuming that the mind won't arrive by itself at its own source. That the mind won't want to think about deity or emptiness. I think that most people who try to write spontaneously, write garbage. I'll agree there.

Student: Well, that's what I'm saying, that perhaps there's a need for more self-conscious . . .

Ginsberg: Well, you better define what you mean by self-conscious.

Student: Well, having the idiom in mind . . .

Ginsberg: You're saying you have to have a presupposition or precontext. Well, I think that would be contrary to this practice, and I think that until you are accomplished in the practice of observing your own mind, and transcribing it, you can't start off with a prefixed idea. Because then you won't observe your mind, you'll be observing the idea and trying to rationally create an extension of the idea or an image to fit things in. Chogyam Trungpa told me something about two years ago which extended something that Kerouac had also said. Kerouac and I were worrying about this problem, trying to formulate it, and he said that if the mind is shapely, the art will be shapely. Or, "Mind is shapely, art is shapely." It's a question of knowing your mind. So the discipline, in a sense, would be having a mind and knowing it. And then when you're writing, that writing will be interesting according to that actual mind.

Student: But the spontaneity is held in a certain form.

Ginsberg: Sometimes. Some spontaneous forms are very formal, like the haiku and the blues. In America, the most extensive practice of spontaneous form is the blues, and calypso, but mostly the blues, and that has a very, very strong form, very definite forms, and that's one of the forms I'd like to teach here—the practical application of blues to Buddhist meditation or something. Anyway, I didn't finish about the other phrase that was a key phrase from 1971 or '72, I guess, here in Boulder. I was writing a spontaneous chain poem with Chogyam and he said, and we finally agreed, "First thought is best thought." That was sort of the formula: first thought, best thought. That is to say, the first thought you had on your mind, the first thought you thought before you thought, yes, you'd have a better thought, before you thought you should have a more formal thought—first thought, best thought. If you stick with first flashes, then you're all right. But the problem is, how do you *get* to that first thought—that's always the problem. The first thought is always the great elevated, cosmic, noncosmic, *shunyata* thought. And then, at least according to the Buddhist formulation, after that you begin imposing names and forms and all that. So it's a question of catching yourself at your first open thought.

Student: Could you give me an example of spontaneity without form?

Ginsberg: Yes, I believe there are examples. I believe Milarepa is an example of spontaneity without form in certain poems. There are certain open poems.

Student: I know, but he was enlightened.

Ginsberg: We're all enlightened. Fuck that bullshit enlightenment. There is no enlightenment. If we're going to start waiting to be enlightened to write poetry . . .

NOTES

[1]Leadbelly's "Boll Weevil Blues."

[2]Chögyam Trumpa, Rimpoche, Tibetan Lama, meditation teacher & poet-calligrapher, founder of Naropa Institute.

[3]It's considered to be bad meditation practice, hanging on greedy for poetic items. A.G. 1979.

AN EXPOSITION OF WILLIAM CARLOS WILLIAMS' POETIC PRACTICE

[This 1975 Naropa lecture was first published in *Loka 2: A Journal from Naropa Institute*, 1976.]

The first scratchings of *Paterson*, his first inspiration—a long speech giving his basic philosophy, where he first lays out that idea, "No ideas but in things," and goes on to illustrate it, is what follows below. He was living around Paterson, in Rutherford, New Jersey, and he decided that he would try and write a monumental *epic* (a poem, according to Pound, which includes history). Paterson was ten miles or so away—Rutherford was a little too small, like a village, Paterson was like a small city, with city history back to the American revolution—Alexander Hamilton founding the tax-free capitalistic Society of Useful Manufacturers, to tap the electric power coming off the great falls in Paterson, second largest waterfall in the North American continent, second only to Niagara. So there was a long history of economic manipulation, or Hamilton versus Jefferson, a major theme in American economic history, which Pound was interested in and turned Williams on to. So Williams decided to use Paterson as an epic center. *(The Collected Earlier Poems*, NY: New Directions, 1966, pp. 233-35)

PATERSON

Before the grass is out the people are out
and bare twigs still whip the wind—
when there is nothing, in the pause between
snow and grass in the parks and at the street ends
— Say it, no ideas but in things—
nothing but the blank faces of the houses
and cylindrical trees

bent, forked by preconception and accident
split, furrowed, creased, mottled, stained
secret—into the body of the light—
These are the ideas, savage and tender
somewhat of the music, et cetera
of Paterson, that great philosopher—

He's making the town into a man, a person with the unconscious of a person, "moving around inside the windows of the buses." So this is his scheme for the whole poem.

From above, higher than the spires, higher
even than the office towers, from oozy fields
abandoned to grey beds of dead grass
black sumac, withered weed stalks
mud and thickets cluttered with dead leaves—
the river comes pouring in above the city
and crashes from the edge of the gorge
in a recoil of spray and rainbow mists—
— Say it, no ideas but in things—
and factories crystallized from its force,
like ice from spray upon the chimney rocks

. . . . . .

Say it! No ideas but in things. Mr.
Paterson has gone away
to rest and write. Inside the bus one sees
his thoughts sitting and standing. His thoughts
alight and scatter—
Who are these people (how complex
this mathematic) among whom I see myself
in the regularly ordered plateglass of
his thoughts, glimmering before shoes and bicycles—?
They walk incommunicado, the
equation is beyond solution, yet
its sense is clear—that they may live
his thought is listed in the Telephone
Directory—

and there's young Alex Shorn
whose dad the boot-black bought a house
and painted it inside

with seascapes of a pale green monochrome—
the infant Dionysus springing from
Apollo's arm—the floors oakgrained in
Balkan fashion— Hermes' nose, the body
of a gourmand, the lips of Cupid, the eyes
the black eyes of Venus' sister—

But who! who are these people? It is
his flesh making the traffic, cranking the car
buying the meat—
Defeated in achieving the solution they
fall back among cheap pictures, furniture
filled silk, cardboard shoes, bad dentistry
windows that will not open, poisonous gin
scurvy, toothache—

. . . . . .

But never, in despair and anxiety
forget to drive wit in, in till it
discover that his thoughts are decorous and simple
and never forget that though his thoughts are decorous
and simple, the despair and anxiety
the grace and detail of
a dynamo—

Divine thought! Jacob fell backwards off the press
and broke his spine. What pathos, what mercy
of nurses (who keep birthday books)
and doctors who can't speak proper english—
is here correctly on a spotless bed
painless to the Nth power—the two legs
perfect without movement or sensation

Twice a month Paterson receives letters
from the Pope, his works are translated
into French, the clerks in the post office
ungum the rare stamps from his packages
and steal them for their children's albums

So in his high decorum he is wise

. . . . . .

What wind and sun of children stamping the snow
stamping the snow and screaming drunkenly
The actual, florid detail of cheap carpet
amazingly upon the floor and paid for
as no portrait ever was— Canary singing
and geraniums in tin cans spreading their leaves
reflecting red upon the frost—
They are the divisions and imbalances
of his whole concept, made small by pity
and desire, they are—no ideas beside the facts—

This is a little essay setting up his major conceptions for a long poem. And coming back over and over again and warning himself *not* to build any large scale poetic system apart from facts or present "ideas" other than "facts." The reason I read this is that the repeated mysterious phrase, "Say it, no ideas but in things," finally turns into his re-definition, "no ideas besides the facts," and is now put down so simply, once and for all, that by this time you must understand it. I remember the first time I heard that phrase I thought, "Now what does that mean?" Would anyone like to explain it?

Student: I was thinking that it means not talking in abstract jargon, philosophy or political explanations. Not to define people in terms of categories.

Ginsberg: If it's *not* that, what *is* it?

Student: Maybe it's to relate to the local specifics that they are handling physically and mentally in the particular.

Student: It's also a question of phenomenology, like when you try to sever the audience from the phenomenon, it becomes sentimentality.

Ginsberg: For those who are involved with philosophical language, I guess that Williams' practice would fall into the area of phenomenology—that is, to study the actual data of the senses.

Student: There's a Zen story about a question a master asked his students. This is the graduation and he has to pass it on to one of his students and he puts a picture on the table, and one student describes the picture, the other one walks up and kicks it off, and he becomes the next master.

Ginsberg: Because he had actual contact with the object, rather than verbal. "The object is a symbol of itself" is what Trungpa has been saying *re* iconography—and Ezra Pound said, "The natural object is always the adequate symbol." Which is saying the same thing as "no ideas but in things."

There are some direct instructions in *Selected Essays* (NY: New Directions Paperbook, 1966) which extend his practice out a little—background to "no ideas but in things." Everybody says "play Zen," everybody says "be grounded," but very few are able to *practice* it. Williams here has actually given you several decades of actual practice in observation and notation, so you know he's sincere, you know he's real, you know he's grounded, he knows what he is doing. If you *study* him, the generalization "no ideas but in things" makes sense. So it's really interesting to see what he has to say when he does make critical generalizations, because he knows what he's practicing. In the "Prologue to *Kora in Hell*," he suggests that if you are "sketching," you are *looking*; as you walk around in Boulder, looking at detail, how do you pick out detail from the general mass of trees, how do you describe one tree out of many trees? His phrasing for that might be "how could you find the true value of that one tree?" Because "The true value is that peculiarity which gives an object a character by itself." *(Selected Essays,* p. 11). I had at one time thought that in that sentence he had given specific directions—to pick out the aspect of a tree which makes it *different* from another tree, and then using that detail to describe the tree. But that was only my interpretation of what Williams said, so I'll claim credit for that invention, for that particular practice! If you want to describe a tree, don't try to describe every atom, and don't try to describe every leaf, or every cut and crinkle in the bark. You have to pick out that aspect of the tree, whether a broken branch or two horn-like limbs at the top that come forth above the leaves, or a cluster of caterpillars' nests in one lower branch, or the "scarlet and pink shoot-tips waving delicately in the breeze" or whatever you want. Whatever detail, whatever "particularity" of the tree that strikes your eye first, or stands out in the tree. The same is true for describing a person, a guy with a big nose with snot hanging down, you've got the whole face there. Most beginning writers have difficulty describing a specific person because they don't know where to begin. They say, well, shall I begin with the shoes, or what? You should begin with either the first grotesque thing that meets your eye or that particular detail of a person, a tree, a train or a car which is most singular at first glance or memory. "The true value is that peculiarity which gives an object a character by itself." That's a sort of direction for how you go about picking out detail. The true value of Allen Ginsberg is that peculiar twist of mind, of voice, which gives me character by myself—like a paralyzed right cheek at the moment.

He was writing in that Prologue about the difficulty of getting people to actually look at their own local detail—because everybody wants to write some sort of "poetry," they tend to look for a gilded aspect of reality. "To me this is the gist of the whole matter. It is easy to fall under the spell of a certain mode, especially if it be remote in origin . . . " (*SE*, p. 11). That's sort of like Donovan's lyrics, or Kahlil Gibran. "It is easy to fall under the spell of a certain mode, especially if it be remote in origin, leaving thus certain of its members essential to a reconstruction of its significance permanently lost in an impenetrable mist of time. But the thing that always stands permanently in the way of good writing is always one: the virtual impossibility of lifting to the imagination those *things which lie under the direct scrutiny of the senses, close to the nose*. [My italics.] It is this difficulty which sets a value upon all works of art, and makes them a necessity." So "no ideas but in things," or "close to the nose."

Student: Can you observe words that way?

Ginsberg: Yes. It relates to something we were talking about before when someone asked me, "Since Williams, what's been accomplished in poetics, what new things have been added?" And we talked about Gertrude Stein's practice of building little sculptures of words. Williams does this occasionally—and he wrote quite a bit about Stein. His idea of what she was doing—and what language can do. He was bugged that the poetry of his time hadn't cleaned itself out from older associations with European language and with European form.

How many here have had some experience with Gertrude Stein or read some Stein? And how many have not? Ah, so the majority *have* now— Anne Waldman was teaching Stein! But I want to give you Williams' apologia for Gertrude Stein, his description of what Stein does (*SE*, pp. 162-63):

It's the disinfecting effect of the Stein manner or better said perhaps, its releasing force, that I wish to dwell upon. It's this which gives a listener to this opera [*Four Saints in Three Acts*, he's reviewing it] his laughs, it's the same thing which fascinates an attentive reader, especially if he knows something about the terrors of writing . . . . For everything we know and do is tied up with words, with the phrases words make, with the grammar which stultifies, the prose or poetical rhythms which bind us to our pet indolences and medievalisms. [Like at the moment, 1975, "Like what's happening, man?" is our medieval indolence of language.] To Americans especially, those who no longer speak English [i.e., those who no longer speak *English* English], this is especially important. We need too often a burst of air in the window of our prose. It is absolutely indispensable that we get this before we can even begin to think straight again. It's the words, the words we need to get back to, words washed clean. Until we get the power of thought back through a new minting of the words we are actually sunk. This is a moral question at base, surely, but a technical one also and first.

But every time anyone today tries to use a word it's like trying to get a few nails out of an old box to fix something with. You have to smash and pull and straighten—and then what have you got? That's not too good a simile, similes never are. In writing you can never pull out the words from the broken wood. They carry everything over with them. Unless—

Stein has gone systematically to work smashing every connotation that words have ever had [This is what you were asking about before, the construction of using words as building blocks without an habitual direct descriptive thing.] in order to get them back clean. It can't be helped that it's been forgotten what words are made for. It can't be helped that the whole house has to come down. In fact the whole house has to come down. It's been proved over and over again. . . . And it has to be rebuilt by unbound thinking. And unbound thinking has to be done with straight, sharp words. Call them nails to hold together the joints of the new architecture.

* * * * * *

Incidentally, on the *Americanist* background, there's the long essay, "America and Alfred Steiglitz," (*SE*, p. 134)—if you want to check into what the common thinking was of all those modernist people hanging around together decades ago in New York. That will give you the main gist of it. Here are a few other piths from *Selected Essays* (pp. 289-91): "The Poem as a Field of Action":

> Now we come to the question of the origin of our discoveries. Where else can what we are seeking arise from but speech? From speech, from American speech as distinct from English speech, or presumably so, if what I say above is correct. In any case (since we have no body of poems comparable to the English) from what we *hear* in America. Not, that is, from a study of the classics, not even the American "Classics"—the *dead* classics which—may I remind you, we have *never heard* as living speech. No one has or can *hear* them as they were written any more than we can *hear* Greek today.
>
> I say this once again to emphasize what I have often said—that we here must *listen* to the language for the discoveries we hope to make . . . .
>
> It is there, in the mouths of the living, that the language is changing and giving new means for expanded possibilities in literary expression and, I add, basic structure—the most important of all.

Thus his prescription for paying attention to actual sound, your own words coming out of your own mouth—like a doctor-scientist classifying, labeling, rearranging rhythms of your own talk, literally going back to the raw material of your own ear.

He was writing here of W. H. Auden, the British poet come to America (who Williams felt didn't quite make it, in this mode, because he still was hearing an English speech). But he was pointing out that Auden came here because he knew the vigor of the speech here as distinct from England—people were actually listening to their own talk. And he was putting down Eliot for that reason, Eliot didn't exploit that possibility.

Now, both on this theme of speech-mindfulness and on the theme of samatha meditation which begins at the end of your nose:

This is a 1939 introduction (*SE*, pp. 233-34) to the assembled works and paintings of Charles Sheeler:

> To be an artist, as to be a good artisan, a man must know his materials. But in addition he must possess that really glandular perception of their uniqueness which realizes in them an end in itself, each piece irreplaceable by a substitute, not to be broken down to other meaning. Not to pull out, transubstantiate, boil, unglue, hammer, melt, digest and psychoanalyze ["I don't want to analyze you . . . mystify you" etc., Bob Dylan 1960s], not even to distill but to see and keep what the understanding touches intact—as grapes are round and come in bunches.
>
> To discover and separate these things from the amorphous, the conglomerate normality with which they are surrounded and of which before the act of "creation" each is a part, calls for an eye to draw out that detail which is in itself the thing, to clinch our insight, that is, our understanding, of it.
>
> It is this eye for the thing that most distinguishes Charles Sheeler—and along with it to know that every hair on every body, now or then, in its minute distinctiveness is the same hair, on every body anywhere, at any time, changed as it may be to feather, quill or scale. [Are you following this? It's very funny. I'll read that little thing again because it's really cute.]
>
> The local is the universal. [THE LOCAL IS THE UNIVERSAL.]
>
> Look! that's where painting begins. A bird, up above, flying, may be the essence of it—but a dead canary, with glazed eye, has no less an eye for that well seen becomes sight and song itself. It is in things that for the artist the power lies, not beyond them. Only where the eye hits does sight occur.

This week someone in class handed me a little poem—perfect illustration of that point:

> The room lies quiet and still.
> His gaze lights on a hair hanging from the lamp
> waving gracefully.

It's a perfect little Williams poem, except in a funny way much lighter, a very late refinement. Everybody get that? Anybody not hear that because they were daydreaming or their minds weren't "clamped down" on objects in present time? Okay, I'll read it one more time.

> The room lies quiet and still.
> His gaze lights on a hair hanging from the lamp
> waving gracefully.

One tiny simple isolated detail—somebody's long hair hanging from a lamp, the guy's in bed? But anyway the room lies quiet and still. Very nicely done: David Cheatham. Okay.

Student: Where Williams says "similes never are . . . good" — they virtually have no place in "no ideas but in things" except they tend to clutter up an image?

Ginsberg: Yeah.

Student: So, you would say for good poetry—

Ginsberg: Of this mode—

Student: Yeah, of this mode. You would leave them out?

Ginsberg: Yeah, it would be more expressed by the action. That is, I think both Pound and Williams felt that. Of course, they use them occasionally, but try to eliminate the word "like" or "as" —that tactical trick of putting two things together by saying "like" or "as." If you can do it by just putting thing-facts together without a linking word, if they actually jump together in the mind, then you got it made. You can make a simile if you don't use "like" or "as." The famous imagist poem by Pound,

> The apparition of these faces in the crowd;
> Petals on a wet, black bough.

"In a Station at the Metro." The point there was that he didn't use "is like" —he said, "The apparition of these faces in the crowd;/ Petals on a wet, black bough." So first they revolted against making use of the additional "like" and "as," the words "like" and "as" which are traditionally used to link anything with anything. So they said if you really want to link things up you got to observe them link themselves up in your mind, you don't "make" a simile.

Student: Are metaphors equally suspect then?

Ginsberg: What's metaphor, I've forgotten.

Student: "Your thighs are apple blossoms."

Ginsberg: Yeah, of course. "Your thighs are apple trees/ whose blossoms touch the sky." And the first thing Williams did was have his wife reply, "Which sky?" He opens his poetic career by questioning that use of metaphor. What they substituted was direct "action," direct observation—of course, that was what Hemingway was doing basically.

Okay. One or two little more presentations by Williams on Pound—since you had some doubtful questions about Pound to begin with (*SE*, pp. 108-112).

> They (the lines) [in Pound] have a character that is parcel of the poem itself. (It is in the small make-up of the lines that the character of the poem definitely comes—and beyond which it cannot go.) [In the small make-up of the lines—not in the grandiose conception but in the little tiny detail work, "*small* make-up of the lines."]
>
> It is (in this case) a master meter that wishes to come of the classic but at the same time to be bent to and to incorporate the rhythm of modern speech.
>
> This is or would be the height of excellence—the efflorescence of a rare mind—turned *to* the world.
>
> It succeeds and not [Remember, talking about Pound's attempt to drag in the classical mind which you objected to— It succeeds and not] —it does and fails.
>
> It is in the minutiae—in the minute organization of the words and their relationships in a composition that the seriousness and value of a work of writing exist—*not* in the sentiments, ideas, schemes portrayed . . . .
>
> The seriousness of a work of art, the belief the author has in it, is that he does generate in it—a solution in some sense of the continuous confusion and barrenness which life imposes in its mutations—(on him who will not create) . . . .
>
> We seek a language which will not be at least a deformation of speech as we know it—but will embody all the advantageous jumps, swiftnesses, colors, movements of the day——

—that will, at least, not exclude language as spoken—all language (present) as spoken.

Pound has attempted an ambitious use of language for serious thought without sequestration (the cloistering of words)—an acceptance—and by his fine ear attempted to tune them—excluding nothing.

So the key thing for Williams' practice and what he likes in Pound is: "We seek a language which will not be at least a deformation of speech as we know it." Write as you talk, the model for the writing is the rhythm and diction of the speech "as we know it." At least that the poetry not be "a deformation of [that] speech." But "will embody all the advantageous jumps" —advantageous jumps of mind! —jumps of syntax, "swiftnesses, colors, movements of the day . . . THAT WILL AT LEAST NOT EXCLUDE LANGUAGE AS SPOKEN—ALL language (present) as spoken." That was actually for those days quite a big serious discovery, both for Pound and for Williams. Same for us now!

Student: The line about Greek being too distant because it's not a spoken language, wouldn't that be putting Pound down?

Ginsberg: It's not a yes/no, black-and-white deal, he's saying Pound is trying to make use of what excellence can be made use of. "It is (in this case) a master meter that wishes to come of the classic but at the same time to be bent to and incorporate the rhythm of modern speech . . . . It succeeds and not—it does and it fails." He's saying the guy has worked on Greek and he's making use of classical vowel-length or quantitative measures coinciding with the time-sound of someone actually talking. Williams once told me, "Pound has a mystical ear" —an ear so fine, so subtle, that he could hear gradations of vowel lengths that other people wouldn't notice and so could balance vowels from line to line, work with vowels as a measure of the line as other people couldn't. So Williams isn't putting him down, he's examining what Pound is trying to do: make a new kind of American measure based on the approximation of classical quantity.

Student: You're referring to the poems that Pound wrote in *Persona*?

Ginsberg: It's Williams' review of *A Draft of XXX Cantos* (1931), the first Cantos. "Pound has attempted an ambitious use of language for serious thought without . . . (the cloistering of words) —an acceptance—and by his fine ear attempted to tune them [to modern use] —excluding nothing." (*SE*, pp. 111-12).

> He has succeeded against himself. He has had difficulties of training to overcome which he will not completely undo—in himself at least—if that were all.
>
> But the words reveal it: white-gathered, sun-dazzle, rock-pool, god-sleight, sea-swirl, sea-break, vine-trunk, vine-must, pin-rack, glass-glint, wave-runs, salmon-pink, dew-haze, blue-shot, green-gold, green-ruddy, eye-glitter, blue-deep, wine-red, water-shift, rose-paleness, wave-cords, churn-stick.
>
> We have, examining the work, successes—great ones—the first molds—clear cut, never turgid, not following the heated trivial—staying cold, "classical" but swift with a movement of thought.
>
> It stands out from almost all other verse by a faceted quality that is not muzzy, painty, wet. It is a dry, clean use of words. Yet look at the words. They are themselves not dead. They have not been violated by "thinking." They have been used willingly by thought.
>
> Imagistic use has entirely passed out of them, there is almost no use of simile, no allegory—the word has been used in its plain sense to represent a thing—remaining thus loose in its context—not gummy—(when at its best)—an objective unit in the design—but alive.
>
> Pound has taken them up—if it may be risked—alertly, swiftly, but with feeling for the delicate living quality in them—not disinfecting, scraping them, but careful of the life. The result is that they stay living—and discreet.
>
> Or almost. [Then he puts him down a little.] For beside living passages, there are places where he wrenches the words about for what "ought to be" their conformation.
>
> [But] That's no matter. He has taken up language and raised it to a height where it may stand—beside Artemis——
>
> If that is not a purpose worthy of a poet and if Pound has not done it—then——
>
> It isn't all, it's even (in a sense) a defect to want so much the Artemis thing. But Pound has lifted the language up as no one else has done—wherever he has lifted it—or what-

ever done to it in the lifting.

His defects (dey's good too) are due to his inability to surmount the American thing—or his ability to do so without physical success—if that be preferred.

Very good criticism of him, very honest, really registers the turns of his mind, a very solid common sense. So what I recommend if you want to know *how* Williams thinks, some of the "Prologue to *Kora in Hell*," probably a little bit on James Joyce, "A Note on the Recent Work of James Joyce" back in 1927, the review of Pound, "Excerpts from a Critical Sketch: *A Draft of XXX Cantos*," "The Work of Gertrude Stein," they're only a few pages each, just little reviews that he wrote for *Contact* magazine, or whoever he was writing for then, *The Nation*. If you want to know about Marianne Moore, his is one of the best essays on Marianne Moore. And the whole "American Background," that long essay on America and Alfred Steiglitz in 1934. And this little "A 1 Pound Stein." Little thing on Sheeler has a little bit more on Americana and imagism. There's a weird review of Carl Sandburg calling his entire range of poetry a featureless desert with interesting poems, but featureless in the sense that in the verse there was no attention paid to the actual composition of verse as speech, so there was no form given to the verse— Williams got more and more interested in some kind of "American measure," or *some* kind of definiteness to the verse forms. Well, there's all these great letters between Pound and Williams. Well, if you want to know how they related, sort of (*SE*, p. 8)—

> . . . God knows I have to work hard enough to escape, not *propagande*, but getting centered in *propagande*. And America? What the h--l do you a blooming foreigner know about the place. Your *père* only penetrated the edge, and you've never been west of Upper Darby, or the Maunchunk switchback.
>
> Would H., with the swirl of the prairie wind in her underwear, or the Virile Sandburg recognize you, an effete easterner as a REAL American? INCONCEIVABLE!!!!!
>
> My dear boy you have never felt the woop of the PEEraries. You have never seen the projecting and protuberant Mts. of the SIerra Nevada. WOT can you know of the country?
>
> You have the naive credulity of a Co. Clare emigrant. But I (*der grosse Ich*) have the virus, the bacillus of the land in my

blood, for nearly three bleating centuries.

(Bloody snob. 'eave a brick at 'im!!!) . . .

I was very glad to see your wholly incoherent un-american poems in the L.R. [*Little Review*]

Of course Sandburg will tell you that you miss the "big drifts," and Bodenheim will object to your not being sufficiently decadent.

You thank your blookin gawd you've got enough Spanish blood to muddy up your mind, and prevent the current American ideation from going through it like a blighted colander.

The thing that saves your work is opacity, and don't forget it. Opacity is NOT an American quality. Fizz, swish, gabble, and verbiage, these are *echt americanisch*.

And alas, alas, poor old Masters. Look at Oct. *Poetry*.

And so forth. This is Pound to Williams—'cause Pound was born in Haley, Idaho, and Williams was just second generation. When Pound ran off to Europe he was a real American running off, whereas Williams had this sort of guilty second generation or third generation, second generation thing of trying—well that's the whole point about Williams, he was a foreigner trying to talk American, he was trying to figure out how people talked, actually. It was his advantage, in a way.

In the early Williams, there's a kind of opaque quality. "To an Old Jaundiced Woman" (*Collected Earlier Poems*, p. 268):

O tongue
licking
the sore on
her netherlip

O toppled belly

O passionate cotton
stuck with
matted hair

elsian slobber
upon
the folded handkerchief

I can't die

—moaned the old
jaundiced woman
rolling her
saffron eyeballs

I can't die
I can't die

That's the doctor taking notes, probably on his prescription pad from the size of the line. Because he did write a lot on his prescription pad. "Elsian!" Elsian is his own personal mythological dumb used slattern servant girl broad who gets tragically fucked up by life. "Some Elsie," some doctor's servant— "her great/ ungainly hips and flopping breasts// addressed to cheap/ jewelry/ and rich young men with fine eyes . . . " "Some Elsie," he says. So he's made an adjective out of it, "elsian slobber." A poem "To Elsie," beginning "The pure products of America/ go crazy" (*CEP*, p. 270-72). That was his presentation of the karmic situation of America, actually: "imaginations which have no// peasant traditions to give them/ character" and

as if the earth under our feet
were
an excrement of some sky

and we degraded prisoners
destined
to hunger until we eat filth

while the imagination strains
after deer
going by fields of goldenrod . . .

Student: Had you read that when you started *Howl*?

Ginsberg: Yes, I had read that—I had that very much in mind when I wrote *Howl*— I'm glad you saw the correlation, it's his understanding of the "imagination." That is, his freedom of imagination, his recognition of the beauteous, hideous necessity of imagination; in imagination at least we're free. If we're stuck and hemmed in by what *seem* to us "facts," still there's the heart's imagination and the mind's imagination of what we actually desire. Here defined as "deer/ going by fields of goldenrod in/ the stifling heat of September . . . " That is out on the open road. But "as if the earth under our feet/ were/ an excrement of some sky// and we degraded prisoners/ destined/ to hunger until we eat filth," seemed to me like the whole karmic condition of America, when I discovered this poem in the fifties.

Another little prophetic turn of sexual imagination, "Horned Purple" (*CEP*, p. 273—74).

> This is the time of year
> when boys fifteen and seventeen
> wear two horned lilac blossoms
> in their caps—or over one ear
> . . . .
> Out of their sweet heads
> dark kisses—rough faces

That's really sweet, the last line, funny thing for him to come to—he finally got the essence of adolescent desirousness, actually the old satyric meaning. Soon after that comes one moment when his attention is totally fixed and concentrated on one object (*CEP*, p. 277).

> so much depends
> upon
>
> a red wheel
> barrow
>
> glazed with rain
> water
>
> beside the white
> chickens

I always figured that "so much depends," means his whole mind depends on the image. Or "so much," a clear apprehension of the entire universe: just being there completely mindful— I heard a fly buzz when I died—that's Emily Dickinson's line.

Student: Your introduction to *Visions of Cody* talked about a karmic hangover in America, what's that mean?

Ginsberg: Somebody lands and deceives the red man and steals his space to begin with. America never did belong to us. So that's why our forefathers were always looking up to English manners and English poetry. Williams finally comes along and has to confront that effect—wrote his long poetic-history book, *In the*

American Grain, wherein recognizing how we took over the actual land by force we therefore got this neurosis of not wanting to *see* the land we had taken, not wanting to actually live here, but wanting to live in a mechanical dream world. With imports from England for thought, meter, poesy, music, philosophy, rather than having to feel the tragic fact that we're trespassers in our own bodies and on our own land. So then Williams was recognizing that fact, urging that we recognize the awkwardness and the weirdness of our presence here, which is why he dug Poe. Thus all his prose poems about other heroes who understood America in his terms.

Student: Similar view to Gary Snyder's *Earth House Hold*?

Ginsberg: Snyder? Well, Williams is one of Snyder's heroes, yeah. I suppose Snyder actually belongs to that lineage, they met actually, turned each other on, and Williams noticed Snyder's poetry later.

In "Rapid Transit" Williams sounds like Philip Whalen (*CEP*, p. 282). (Actually compare this with a poem in the Don Allen anthology by Whalen, "Big High Song for Somebody.") "Rapid Transit":

> Somebody dies every four minutes
> in New York State—
>
> To hell with you and your poetry—
> You will rot and be blown
> through the next solar system
> with the rest of the gases—
>
> What the hell do you know about it?
>
> AXIOMS
>
> Don't get killed
>
> Careful Crossing Campaign
> Cross Crossings Cautiously
>
> . . . .
>
> Interborough Rapid Transit Co.

That particular poem probably influenced Whalen—randomness and the humor, composing out of the subway map and subway signs.

"The Descent of Winter" (p. 297) is a classic exercise again in "sketching" like the one we had on "Sunday" (p. 109). Trungpa suggested taking a walk in Boulder and watching rather than analyzing details, and then I read, following that, Williams' series of simple sketches. Here he's a little older, with a series of clever vignettes—little fragments, he's not even trying to finish a poem any more, just trying to get a little detail. There's no hope in writing unless you can accumulate many many tiny details, tiny shells of coral accumulate, an island slowly forming, to wait for others to drop their shit on it and make it habitable. You know, he's saying you have to build up an entire poetic universe of detail. "and there's a little blackboy/ in a doorway/ scratching his wrists/ . . . " So that's as far as he'd gotten by the last line "October tenth/ 1927" (p. 299).

> In the dead weeds a rubbish heap
> aflame . . .
> . . . .
> What chance have the old? . . .
> . . . .
> Their feet hurt, they are weak
> they should not have to suffer
> as younger people must and do
> there should be a truce for them.

The object there is his own compassionate thoughts about old folks.

Jumping to page 303.

> 11/1
>
> The moon, the dried weeds
> and the Pleiades—
>
> Seven feet tall
> the dark, dried weedstalks
> make a part of the night
> a red lace
> on the blue milky sky
>
> Write—
> by a small lamp
>
> the Pleiades are almost

nameless
and the moon is tilted
and halfgone

And in runningpants and
with ecstatic, aesthetic faces
on the illumined
signboard are leaping
over printed hurdles and
"¼ of their energy comes from bread"

two
gigantic highschool boys
ten feet tall

A bread advertisement, it's a very funny combo: a billboard advertisement off a highway in New Jersey surrounded by dried weeds.

Student: Did he get turned on by photography, by stills?

Ginsberg: Yeah, that's why he was hanging around with Alfred Steiglitz. He probably, I think, took that as a form, sketching or still photography. What I like are the almost minimal little sketch details because they're sort of the vipasyana practice that anybody can do. And occasionally then there'll be some burst of a larger ambition like on page 308:

11/8

O river of my heart polluted
and defamed I have compared you
to that other lying in
the red November grass
beginning to be cleaned now
from factory pollution

Though at night a watchman
must still prowl lest some paid hand
open the waste sluices—

That river will be clean
before ever you will be

Student: Couldn't you say then why not take a photograph of it?

Ginsberg: Well, because you're beginning, you're practicing with language, to see if you can build a coral island out of all the little details. To see if you can train yourself in speech consciousness. You're practicing a speech consciousness, not an eyeball consciousness. Photography would be an eyeball consciousness. The poem would be speech consciousness, a refinement of *speech*.

Student: (inaudible: . . . "Camera" . . . "framing?")

Ginsberg: Framing, definitely, framing your *mind* in this case, framing the language of your mind. You remember way at the very beginning he dipped his hand in the "filthy Passaic" and the Passaic River in Paterson consented to him being the muse of the river and years later, 1927, "Oh river of my heart polluted . . . that river will be . . . " Talking about the river of my heart.

But then there's a funny outburst, more like 1960s. He gets political, the Sacco/Vanzetti case. A thing called "Impromptu: the Suckers" (p. 315), which is a really prophetic sort of anti-police-state radical rant for Williams, very "vulgar" for Williams. Full of energy and full of good intentions, and information actually; what's interesting is the straightforward citizenly stubborn toughness here. The "sucker" is the entire nation at this point, the guys who voted for Nixon or the guys who voted for or were in favor of executing two anarchist fellows accused of a bomb plot, Nicolo Sacco and Bartolemeo Vanzetti.

IMPROMPTU: THE SUCKERS

Take it out in vile whisky, take it out
in lifting your skirts to show your silken
crotches; it is this that is intended.
You are it. Your pleas will always be denied.
You too will always go up with the two guys,
scapegoats to save the Republic and
especially the State of Massachusetts. The
Governor says so and you ain't supposed
to ask for details.

Your case has been reviewed by
  high-minded
and unprejudiced observers (like hell
they were!) the president of a great
university; the president of a noteworthy

technical school and a judge too old to sit
on the bench, men already rewarded for
their services to pedagogy and the enforcement
of arbitrary statutes. In other words
pimps to tradition—

Why in hell didn't they choose some other
kind of "unprejudiced adviser" for their
death council? instead of sticking to that
autocratic strain of Boston backwash, except
that the council was far from unprejudiced
but the product of a rejected, discredited
class long since outgrown except for use in
courts and school, and that they
wanted it so—

Why didn't they choose at least one decent
Jew or some fair-minded Negro or anybody
but such a triumvirate of inversion, the
New England aristocracy, bent on working off
a grudge against you, Americans, you
are the suckers, you are the ones who will
be going up on the eleventh to get the current
shot into you, for the glory of the state
and the perpetuation of abstract justice—

And all this in the face of the facts: that
the man who swore, and deceived the jury
wilfully by so doing, that the bullets found
in the bodies of the deceased could be
identified as having been fired from the pistol
of one of the accused—later
acknowledged that he could not so identify
them; that the jurors now seven years after
the crime do not remember the details and
have wanted to forget them; that the
prosecution has never succeeded in
apprehending the accomplices nor in connecting
the prisoners with any of the loot stolen—

The case is perfect against you, all the

documents say so—in spite of the fact that
it is reasonably certain that you were not
at the scene of the crime, shown, quite as
convincingly as the accusing facts in the
court evidence, by better reasoning to have
been committed by someone else with whom
the loot can be connected and among whom the
accomplices can be found—

It's no use, you are Americans, just the dregs.
It's all you deserve. You've got the cash,
what the hell do you care? You've got
nothing to lose. You are inheritors of a great
tradition. My country right or wrong!
You do what you're told to do. You don't
answer back the way Tommy Jeff did or Ben
Frank or Georgie Washing. I'll say you
don't. You're civilized. You let your
betters tell you where you get off. Go
ahead—

But after all, the thing that swung heaviest
against you was that you were scared when
they copped you. Explain that you
nature's nobleman! For you know that every
American is innocent and at peace in his
own heart. He hasn't a damned thing to be
afraid of. He knows the government is for
him. Why, when a cop steps up and grabs
you at night you just laugh and think it's
a hell of a good joke—

This is what was intended from the first.
So take it out in your rotten whisky and
silk underwear. That's what you get out of
it. But put it down in your memory that this
is the kind of stuff that they can't get away
with. It is there and it's loaded. No one
can understand what makes the present age
what it is. They are mystified by certain
insistences.

Well, that's like a great tirade, a model for dealing right now with the Wounded Knee trial or any of the recent "dissident" conspiracy trials, present police-state situations. And Williams' take on it, with all the details of the Sacco/Vanzetti case and then his peroration including case-facts, his energy on it is one of the few great political common sense breakthroughs, I mean it's also *vulnerable* Williams getting mad and angry like a good citizen. A funny model poem with weird prophetic seriousness— "Why when a cop steps up and grabs/ you at night you just laugh and think it's/ a hell of a good joke—" I always thought this was a really amazing poem for him, following "The pure products of America/ go crazy," those two. Apparently at this time he got prophetic about America.

Student: What do you think about the form of that? 'Cause it's very interesting in that sense, broken down as a set of paragraphs.

Ginsberg: I bet you it was written in prose and he chopped it up, it'd be interesting to know. It looks like, oh, blank verse, just the eye on the page makes it look like blank verse. Of course, the actual speech is much more variable than Shakespeare's blank verse. I don't know how he arrived at this, it's one of the very first pieces of that kind, with a thick line. Except "A Morning Imagination of Russia" and the other thing I read from *Paterson* originally, is where he gets philosophical. "No ideas but in things" has the same form—a thick line on the page, 'cause he's got a lot to say, a lot of talking to do.

That was the one thing that turned me on to my own style, I think it's one of the grosser elements in Williams, but it's also one of the most charming things he did, that he let himself open and he laid out that sort of vulnerable angry tirade. It also shows you a tradition, there was a breakthrough in consciousness in America all the way back then in the late twenties and the early thirties, of this kind of police-state paranoia, heavy metal Burroughsian awareness. It was pretty strong then among anarchists, among the literary bohemians of that day. That radical awareness of the difference between a political front as presented by judges and university trustees, and what was actually going on in the back room of courts and jails. It's amazing how solid his perception is there and how valid it is now.

That long poem of Williams' was a political statement, a sudden angry testament prophetic of later police-state tendencies in America. The Sacco/Vanzetti case: two Italian fish peddlers from Boston were set up, on a fake bombing charge, and executed. It was the first blood in this era of state murder at the beginning of the Great Cold War. It was a *big* thing, all the intellectuals got involved including Williams, it was one of the big causes of the radical left.

Student: Woody Guthrie did an album of a lot of songs about it.

Ginsberg: Yeah. There were songs, books, poems, my father wrote a poem that was in *The New Masses*. Edna St. Vincent Millay wrote a poem called "Justice Denied in Massachusetts" once they were killed.

That political strain comes into Williams—there's a description of the Capitol building in Washington, his aesthetic comment on the vision of America conjured by a collage of elements—paintings, sculpture, architectural construction—at Washington Capitol (*CEP*, p. 325-28): "It Is a Living Coral// a trouble// archaically fettered/ to produce . . . dead// among the wreckage/ sickly green." That was his "character" of the Capitol; a national portrait done in the official detail using the architecture of the Capitol building: as near as you could get, if you were an imagist using "no ideas but in things" and wanting to do a commentary on the state of the nation.

More into his real genre, "Hemmed-in Males" (p. 322); it's one that I always thought was like the best of poor old Paterson or Rutherford. "The saloon is gone up the creek/ . . . there's no place// any more for me to go now/ except home—" Real sympathetic and sweet. "You can laugh at him without his/ organs but that's the way with/ a river when it wants to/ drown you . . . "

A little exercise called "Florida, 1924," (p. 329) gets back to his preoccupation with finding little rhythmical turns in his own speech usable as poetry. The theme is his imagination wandering off while he's in the real Florida doing a real job; actually, dreaming of Florida while doing his job there as a doctor. But listening to the sounds. The very last line is classic American speech, one of the lines he thought was rhythmically most interesting. It has the rhythm *-da-da-da da-da-da-da-da-da / da-da*. You'll recognize it when you get to it. "This Florida, 1924 . . ./ Peggy has a little albumen/ in hers—" Actually, so he's got this long disquisition on "orange" — "Rather, hibiscus,/ let me examine/" 'Cause he's doing his pees, examining all the little pee samples to see who's got what, kidney trouble. "Peggy has a little albumen/ in hers—" That's the last phrase of the poem.

Now the great poem on the tree. Remember I paraphrased the *Kora in Hell* Prologue in order to describe one tree of all the trees on earth, to separate out that one tree that you want to describe (if you're trying to write a song lyric and you want to put in something real sharp, a visual image, that people will remember, or poem) you have to rely on the specific detail that differs it from all objects of its kind. And his most interesting tree I think is "Young Sycamore." You completely see a tree with a number of little details, I think it's the acme of tree description. Randall Jarrell noticed that Williams was really conversant with trees, remember, "The trees/ are become/ beasts fresh-risen/ from the sea—" Jarrell said Williams has turned more people into trees (or more trees into people, whichever)—than any other poet. Odd, that Williams, supposed to be this "difficult modernist," was actually so well connected with old-fashioned pastoral nature. "Young Sycamore" (p. 332) begins really nice. "I must tell you." "I must tell you." The doctor in his office, "I must tell you." Who is he talking to? You, actually. "I must tell *you*, this young tree . . . " And it's all one fast notation, probably three breaths I would say. There are only two, well maybe one two three four five breaths, I would guess. I'll try reading it again with five breaths according to his scoring.

YOUNG SYCAMORE

I must tell you
this young tree
whose round and firm trunk
between the wet

pavement and the gutter
(where water
is trickling) rises
bodily

into the air with
one undulant
thrust half its height—

and then

dividing and waning
sending out
young branches on
all sides—

hung with cocoons
it thins
till nothing is left of it
but two

eccentric knotted
twigs
bending forward
hornlike at the top

That's the right way. He's given the scoring, there's a little parenthesis which requires another breath after "half its height—" there's another dash after "young branches on/ all sides—" and from "hung with cocoons" to end "hornlike at the top" it's all one breath. So there's a lot going on in these stanzas which are relatively even four-line stanzas, the poem is arranged into four line parts.

Here's a funny little photograph at home called "Poem"—obviously it's something he noticed and wrote down, realized later was a poem, so he called it a "Poem" (p. 340).

As the cat
climbed over
the top of

the jamcloset
first the right
forefoot

carefully
then the hind
stepped down

into the pit of
the empty
flowerpot

It's mostly a line of three syllables each. In one stanza the first line is "the jamcloset" which is four, but then the third and last line of that stanza is only two syllables, so he balanced it out. Are you following me? It's basically a line of three syllables. And if you're writing any kind of short-line poetry like that, counting syllables is one good way to base your line. It gives you a funny little regularity, funny measure, almost unconscious, you wouldn't notice it unless you were interested in trying to find out what's going on. But it does give a kind of backbone. Not yet the variable foot, you see. Does everybody follow what I'm saying about counting syllables? (Marianne Moore was the great lady of syllable count.)

My father's favorite Williams poem, page 342:

> THE JUNGLE
>
> It is not the still weight
> of the trees, the
> breathless interior of the wood,
> tangled with wrist-thick
>
> vines, the flies, reptiles,
> the forever fearful monkeys
> screaming and running
> in the branches—
>
> but
>
> a girl waiting
> shy, brown, soft-eyed—
> to guide you
> Upstairs, sir.

And then, like a Chinese poem (except a Chinese poet compares the fallen lotus blossom floating down the river to the fading away of charm of cheek of his lady), Williams going from ward to ward of the Paterson General Hospital had other flowers or blossoms to observe, here in "Between Walls" (p. 343).

> the back wings
> of the
>
> hospital where
> nothing

will grow lie
cinders

in which shine
the broken

pieces of a green
bottle

With Chinese poetry in mind, that tradition of observation, he's looked into that back-ass place of every building that everybody knows from working as a secretary in trucking companies to going to high school too late. So he's comparing that green bottle to the living flower—of his imagination or of his perception. Phil, you have something relevant?

Student: Well, I was thinking of the other poem. I wondered if every word was absolutely necessary and weighted and considered, right? He goes off on this discursive thing . . .

Ginsberg: Yes, 'cause it's not a real jungle he's talking about, this guy is talking about an imaginary jungle. So he's got "forever fearful monkeys screaming" and so on. That's obviously an exaggeration. When he gets to what he actually sees, "but/ a girl waiting . . . sir" that's where he gets more precise. The actual description of the jungle is like a bullshit jungle. But he's also saying the *real* jungle of emotions where you're trapped by wild beasties is the actual everyday situation, not the imaginary jungle in the Amazon that you read about in W.H. Hudson or can imagine from the movies. So he's got a movie jungle there with naturally imprecise sloppy language a little bit, he's never been in the jungle.

Student: Well, I liked it myself. I'm just saying that that kind of throws another light on what Pound was . . .

Ginsberg: Yeah, but I'm just pointing out that he's talking about an imaginary jungle, that it's not an observed jungle, and that everybody's scared of imaginary jungles but the *real* jungle they see in front of them is the considerable one. Obviously, that's not like a practice trip, that description of the jungle with wrist-thick vines is very vague, "flies and reptiles," pretty much a Rutherford jungle, isn't a jungle of somebody who's really been around a jungle.

In "Nantucket" (p. 348) there's a little portrait, not of a person but a room with all the perfect nostalgia of a specific room.

> Flowers through the window
> lavender and yellow
>
> changed by white curtains—
> Smell of cleanliness—
>
> Sunshine of late afternoon—
> On the glass tray
>
> a glass pitcher, the tumbler
> turned down, by which
>
> a key is lying— And the
> immaculate white bed

That's real New England island—perfect boarding house. And well, yeah, the poem I like best to illustrate his method is something he left literally as a note for his wife, which after he reread in the morning he put in the book as another poem (p. 354).

> THIS IS JUST TO SAY
>
> I have eaten
> the plums
> that were in
> the icebox
>
> and which
> you were probably
> saving
> for breakfast
>
> Forgive me
> they were delicious
> so sweet
> and so cold

I think that's one of his greatest exemplary poems, 'cause finally it's where life and poetry are identical, there's no separation, that the note that he would write to communicate to his wife is identical to what he would put in a book to communicate to the eternal.

Student: . . . see everything as poetry?

Ginsberg: Well, everything *is* poetry, to begin with, if you see it. He begins to *see* everything finally. And naturally it becomes poetry. Which is the point, again—making a parallel to the lectures going on upstairs, on the iconography of Buddhism, where the upstairs guru is pointing out that if you *look*, and if you're attentive without resentment, every noise becomes punctuation in the big mantra and every little movement has a meaning of its own. (You know that old song, [singing] "Every little movement has a meaning of its own" about the belly dancers of the vampish twenties, you know.)

Yeah, so there's a point, as Rinpoche was pointing out, where one's perception of everyday life becomes clear because there's no obstacle of trying to impose a thought on it, or there's no obstacle trying to impose a poem on it. No obstacle trying to impose another world on it. So that it becomes a complete absolute world in which "the natural object is always an adequate symbol" of itself and in which every object shines out with its own significance, a meaning to which every movement has relationship—the example Trungpa'd given was the ground insects in the parking lot, some twirling around, some zigzagging, some going in a straight line, some eventually stopping and going off on a tangent. They all follow their own self-ultimate fatal paths and an observant person seeing them would be struck by the humor and curiosity of so much individuality finding its own way. Or a person wanting to impose an idea would say, "That's nothing but a bunch of insects, why bother to look at them, why bother perceiving them?" And about some cold plums in the icebox, what's so poetic about that? But the clarity and preciseness of the perception as well as the humor and generosity of his relationship with his wife, revealed by the tone and exactness of the note that he sends her, makes it a picture of their entire domestic life and psychological relationship. That she got these plums which she says, "Save for breakfast, don't take in the middle of the night." And him knowing and saying, "which you were probably saving for breakfast, forgive me." He's stolen the plums from his wife, "Forgive me/ they were delicious." So you have their sexual relationship set up actually by that little thing. I mean you have their personal, emotive, role-playing set-up and then you have the doctor who's coming down in the middle of the night (as in the early poem noticing "a glass filled with parsley—crisp green . . . on the grooved drain-board" and standing there in his pajamas and turning on the spigot and waiting for the water to freshen before it gets nice and cold for his drink. Noticing how the water "freshens.") So there's a doctor in the kitchen again, but totally awake with beating mind, "Forgive me/ they were delicious/ so sweet/ and so cold." Or, actually he was probably just tired and wrote it down, but in the morning he realized how precise the writing was.

* * * * *

Well, same time, same mental station, same movement, the Imagists based their practice on direct observation of the image. People also included their thought or feelings as part of the hard data of Objectivist movement. Another group called Activist used language that was sharp-edged, "active" rather than vague and passive. Imagists, Objectivists, Activists, various metamorphoses of the same notion of "direct treatment of the object—" as in Pound's phrase.

Number 19 of a series called "Five Groups of Verse" —poems by Charles Reznikoff first published in 1927 (*By the Waters of Manhattan*, NY: New Directions Paperbook, 1962, p. 8).

> She sat by the window opening into the airshaft,
> and looked across the parapet
> at the new moon.
>
> She would have taken the hairpins out of her carefully
> coiled hair,
> and thrown herself on the bed in tears;
> but he was coming and her mouth had to be pinned
> into a smile.
> If he would have her, she would marry whatever he was.
>
> A knock. She lit the gas and opened her door.
> Her aunt and the man—skin loose under his eyes, the
> face slashed with wrinkles.
> "Come in," she said as gently as she could and smiled.

That's so complete, and right into the heart, because it's a whole lifetime and a lifetime that's one thing, but a lifetime of feeling compressed there—generous feeling and realistic situation-appreciation—" 'Come in,' she said as gently as she could and smiled." So that the subject of the poem is as intelligent and as sentient as we are—and Reznikoff seems like a very solid, tearful man. There's a few like this. Number 25 of the series: one that I like almost the most, it's just totally perfect detail, totally perfectly composed seamless no comment but the detail (Reznikoff, p. 11).

> The shoemaker sat in the cellar's dusk beside his bench and sewing-machine, his large, blackened hands, finger tips flattened and broad, busy.
> Through the grating in the sidewalk over his window, paper and dust were falling year by year.
>
> At evening Passover would begin. The sunny street was crowded. The shoemaker could see the feet of those who walked over the grating.
> He had one pair of shoes to finish and he would be through.
> His friend came in, a man with a long, black beard, in shabby, dirty clothes, but with shoes newly cobbled and blacked.
> "Beautiful outside, really the world is beautiful."
>
> A pot of fish was boiling on the stove. Sometimes the water bubbled over and hissed. The smell of the fish filled the cellar.
> "It must be beautiful in the park now. After our fish we'll take a walk in the park." The shoemaker nodded.
> The shoemaker hurried his work on the last shoe. The pot on the stove bubbled and hissed. His friend walked up and down the cellar in shoes newly cobbled and blacked.

It's that fish hissing on the stove, so that you know that the fish is going to hiss-burn on the black stove with an extra fishy smell in the basement full of leather smell to begin with. I mean it's so totally of the earth and of human existence on the earth, samsaric, the poem's a triumph and it's composed of all these totally humble details. I mean everybody else would have thrown it away, no poetry at all, totally impossible to deal with.

I want to finish now with a little Williams, summing it all up—the effort that both Reznikoff and Williams were making—"Birds and Flowers" —so suggesting a still life (pp. 356-57).

> Nothing is lost! The white
> shellwhite
> glassy, linenwhite, crystalwhite

crocuses with orange centers
the purple crocus with
an orange center, the yellow
crocus with a yellow center—

. . . .

Though the eye
turns inward, the mind
has spread its embrace—in
a wind that
roughs the stiff petals—
More! the particular flower is
blossoming . . .

So—that's what they were all trying to do, get that particular flower of perception blossoming in America, a whole phalanx of writers trying to find an American Language, using American local diction, trying to find the rhythms of their own talk, "Peggy has a little albumen in hers," ah, trying to compose poems that are indistinguishable from our ordinary speech, and working with perceptions that are indistinguishable from the actual perceptions of our ordinary mind; but which when recognized, and appreciated consciously, transform the entire feeling of existence to a totally new sympathetic universe where we're at home, where we're playful, where we're generous, because the mind overflows with its perceptions, and the perceptions are all generous because they're not blocked by anger. Actually the beginning of this poetic alchemy, as Williams says, is: "A new world is only a new mind." And a new mind is only new words. Or a new mind in poetics is only a new set of words equivalent to those you're actually able to use with your mouth when you're talking—so you don't twist your mouth, and twist your brain, and twist your so-called soul, to strain for an effect of a universe that isn't there, but are talking plainly about what you see in front of you that is there. In that way you don't create paranoia, you dispel paranoia, because you are reaffirming, through clearly presenting your perceptions, the very same perceptions in the minds and eyes of others. So that finally it does come down to what Plato originally said— "When the mode of music changes, the walls of the city shake." When the mode, here of prosody, returns to its normal order, there then begins a new direct perception in the soul, so that "noble is changed to no bull," so that you can see through hallucinated language, you have something to compare hallucinated language with, and you can tell what language rises out of direct contact with phenomena as distinct from language that rises from overheated imagination or desire-to-impress by writing something sounding "poetical." Williams becomes a standard for morality, in a sense, or for a normal state of mind, a standard you can measure your own perceptions and sanity against, measure your own poetry against, measure your own glimpses of what you see, what you recognize of what you see. Thus actually Williams is the true hero of the first half of the American Century, carrying on the work of Whitman.

SOME DIFFERENT CONSIDERATIONS IN MINDFUL ARRANGEMENT OF OPEN VERSE FORMS ON THE PAGE

1. Count of syllables (Marianne Moore, Kenneth Rexroth) (Creeley's mono syllabics)
2. Count of accents (Traditional iambic etc. foot)
3. Measurement of vowel length or quantity (Classical Greek & Latin, Swinburne experiments, Pound, Campion)
4. Recurrent variations of pitch, or "tone leading of vowels"
5. Breath stop (Creeley, Olson, Williams) (new breath, new line) (pause)
6. Units of mouth phrasing (pause within the same breath) (Ginsberg, Olson)
7. Divisions of mental ideas (Corso, Williams)
8. Typographical topography (aesthetic balances on page, symmetry, asymmetry)
9. Heartbeat (Duncan)
10. Conditions of original notation (line-length, verse length, bloc-shape) & writing materials (pocket notebook, booksize journal page, napkin, tape, typewriter, matchbook etc.) (Olson, Ginsberg, etc. Kerouac especially)
11. Chance (arbitrary choice, impulse, fatigue, accident, interruption, sudden impatience or energy)

"Form" is what happens. All considerations are elements of a single "discipline" which is MINDFULNESS or conscious appreciation and awareness of the humours of line arrangements on the page, intelligence in relation to the mental conception of the poem and its vocalization.

Allen Ginsberg, Prepared for
Jack Kerouac School of Disembodied Poetics
Naropa Institute, 1975-1977
April 2, 1977

GREY FOX BOOKS

Guy Davenport
Herakleitos and Diogenes

Edward Dorn
Selected Poems

Allen Ginsberg
The Gates of Wrath: Rhymed Poems 1948–1952
Gay Sunshine Interview (with Allen Young)
Composed on the Tongue

Jack Kerouac
Heaven & Other Poems

Michael McClure
Hymns to St. Geryon & Dark Brown

Frank O'Hara
Early Writing
Poems Retrieved
Standing Still and Walking in New York

Charles Olson
The Post Office

Michael Rumaker
A Day and a Night at the Baths

Gary Snyder
He Who Hunted Birds in His Father's Village: The Dimensions of a Haida Myth

Gary Snyder, Lew Welch & Philip Whalen
On Bread & Poetry

Jack Spicer
One-Night Stand & Other Poems

Lew Welch
How I Work as a Poet & Other Essays/Plays/Stories
I, Leo—An Unfinished Novel
I Remain: The Letters of Lew Welch & the Correspondence of His Friends
Ring of Bone: Collected Poems 1950–1971
Selected Poems
Trip Trap (with Jack Kerouac & Albert Saijo)

Philip Whalen
Decompressions: Selected Poems
Scenes of Life at the Capital